Samuel R. Steel, Jr.
Christmas 1988

America's New Railroads

Also by **Robert S. Carper:**

Focus: The Railroad in Transition

America's New Railroads

Robert S. Carper

SAN DIEGO • NEW YORK
A. S. BARNES & COMPANY, INC.
IN LONDON:
THE TANTIVY PRESS

The Tantivy Press
Magdalen House
136-148 Tooley Street
London, SE1 2TT, England

First Edition
Manufactured in the United States of America
For information write to A. S. Barnes and Company, Inc.,
P.O. Box 3051, San Diego, CA 92038

Library of Congress Cataloging in Publication Data

Carper, Robert S
America's new railroads.

Includes index.
1. Railroads—United States. I. Title.
HE2751.C27 385'.0973 77-84563
ISBN 0-498-02179-1

1 2 3 4 5 6 7 8 9 84 83 82 81 80

To My Wonderful Family . . .
Fern, Pam, and Bruce

Contents

Preface

One of the pitfalls of journalistic writing is that it becomes outdated very rapidly. Scarcely a year after my first work, *Focus: The Railroad in Transition,* appeared on the bookshelves, there arose the recurring stories that marked the economic disaster of the Penn Central. *Focus: The Railroad in Transition* ended in that unique period of time when economists, businessmen, government officials, and many lay people had given their blessing to the wedding of the New York Central and the Pennsylvania Railroad. Thus, *America's New Railroads* takes up where *Focus: The Railroad in Transition* leaves off.

America's New Railroads, unlike *Focus: The Railroad in Transition,* is not a historical chronicle; it is a more pictorially oriented work, containing detailed captions which, taken as a whole, move the reader through the historical period covered by the book. One can see the erosion of the Penn Central, followed by the comparably healthy operations of the two competing roads, the Chessie and the Norfolk and Western. The resurgence of the passenger train also follows a historical sequence. With Conrail, this pictorial essay depicts something that most likely will have vanished by the time this book is on the shelves—the mixture of the locomotives of at least ten railroads, all over the Conrail network. Such a collection of mixed motive power will probably never appear again.

Acknowledgments

Assembling the photographs for this book would have been too great a task for one photographer alone. Supplementing the work of my own camera are the photographs of six top railroad photographers: John Taibi of West Brentwood, New York; Dick Herbert of Wyckoff, New Jersey; John Gabriel of Lansdale, Pennsylvania; Tom Hildreth of Springfield, Massachusetts; Leonard Dunman of Louisville, Kentucky; and Howard Ameling of Fremont, Ohio. Without the excellent work of these photographers, many of whom sat out in freezing cold and other unfavorable weather conditions, this book could not have come together. I would like also to thank the publicity departments and staffs of Conrail, Amtrak, and Auto-Train for the photographs, literature, and technical assistance which they contributed. In particular, a special note of thanks goes to the staff and management of Auto-Train for their hospitality while I was photographing operations at their Lorton terminal.

Introduction

During the period from 1967 to 1977 changes occurred in American railroading that were even more profound than the passing of the steam locomotive and the virtual elimination of the passenger train. In this period, events took place that nearly paralyzed the railroad system in America's industrial heartland and that necessitated large-scale federal intervention to keep the trains running. The years from 1967 to 1978 saw the financial collapse of an American railroad corporation—a collapse of a magnitude never before witnessed in the entire history of our country. This period also saw the cessation of intercity passenger service—which the railroads had offered ever since their creation—to be replaced by a new corporation, the National Railroad Passenger Corporation, better known as Amtrak. A completely new idea in passenger train service grew up in the format of yet another corporation, Auto-Train. Two of the established railroads in the Middle Atlantic–Northeast states—the Chessie System and the Norfolk and Western—had also been created by merger, but, unlike the comatose Penn Central, had posted profits year after year. These railroad systems were now getting ready to assimilate huge blocks of the fallen railroad empire in the Northeast. In this setting, the Consolidated Rail Corporation—Conrail—was created.

Out of this transition has resulted one of the most spectacular panoramas ever to unfold on the miles of rail network within the Midwest and Northeast. The creation of Conrail brought together the locomotives of six different railroads, and it was an everyday occurrence to see trains roar by with diesel units representing a mixture of these now-defunct railroads that now were absorbed by Conrail. The traditional railroad passenger car that once was a part of the fleet of luxury streamliners could be seen parked away on some deserted railroad siding, riddled with bullet holes, while their new sleek Amfleet replacements became the vanguard of Amtrak's new look. The new locomotives that Amtrak placed into service on the Northeast Corridor all sported heavy iron grillwork on their windshields to prevent rock-throwing vandals from turning a railroad engineer into a blind man. Near East Greenwich, R.I., a quarter-mile-long track-laying machine was busy at work converting a part of the old New Haven line into a concrete-tied, high-speed roadbed. The new version of the Turbo-train, created in France, could be seen racing along the old Water Level Route of the New York Central, with names such as the *Empire State Express* and the *DeWitt Clinton*—names that once adorned some of the Central's crack streamliners. In Harrisburg, Pa., a train watcher could see Conrail freights running north, south, east, or west, and occasionally, a yellow-and-blue Chessie locomotive would slip into Rutherford Yard at the head of a run-through freight. In Bellevue, Ohio, a train watcher could see so much Union Pacific and Southern Pacific motive power moving along the route of the Norfolk and Western that he honestly could believe he was out west, not in the State of Ohio. And in Chicago, all of the classic railroad stations that had seen so many of the name streamliners arrive and depart were now closed down, except for one—Union Station. Here, all of Amtrak's operations came to a single, central hub, a far cry from the passenger train heyday of the 1950s. In the Civil War town of Harper's Ferry, W.Va., the sleek Amfleet passenger trains of Amtrak glided over the 100-year-old bridge spanning the Potomac River, while, in the other direction, a heavy coal train blasted eastward through the tunnel on its way to Brunswick, Md., and the port of Baltimore.

This is the picture that is America's New Railroads . . . some of the new, still some of the old, and some of it rooted deep in the past. To this day, many rail fans, some of whom have never seen a steam locomotive in their lives, come out by the hundreds whenever there is a rail excursion like the *Chessie Special* or the Southern's 4501. In the quiet New England town of Ware, Mass. the once-a-week Conrail local is greeted by small children as it drones in to switch cars in the local lumberyard. In the Bicentennial year of 1976, every railroad, large and small, painted at least one of their locomotives in a brilliant red, white, and blue star-spangled color scheme to celebrate the nation's 200th birthday. In Little Rock and in Chattanooga, in Pittsford, N.Y., and in Allston, Mass., railroad stations that had long since seen their last passenger train were now converted into thriving commercial enterprises. In every major city in the country, a commercial restaurant chain called Victoria Station does it one step better: it builds restaurants that look like British railway stations out of old American boxcars and cabooses.

In the pages that follow, the milestone events of the period from 1967 to 1978 are captured as they appeared on the many miles of rail routes centered in the Northeast. They present a vivid photographic chronicle of the railroad systems that have evolved during this period and of America's nostalgic recollection of the past . . . truly, America's New Railroads.

America's New Railroads

1

The Decline and Fall of the Penn Central

On January 18, 1968, the Supreme Court gave the go-ahead to the largest railroad merger in American history. On that date, the New York Central and the Pennsylvania railroads became a single entity, known as the Penn Central Transportation Company. Scarcely five years later, the Penn Central became not only bankrupt, but also insolvent, to the point where it was faced with a shutdown of its entire system. This merger, which was intended to reduce the duplication of services, alleviate the cost of transporting freight and passengers, and create a revived railroad facility for the economically troubled Northeast, became a national disaster. Suddenly, the industrial and economic system of the major part of our nation was faced with paralysis.

What happened?

Although all of the pre-merger economic studies and advertising propaganda hailed the merger as one of the most beneficial moves that ever advanced the status of American railroading, particularly in the Northeast, the differences between the two roads were so great that, right from the start, problems arose. From the executive boardrooms right down to trackside, the Pennsylvania and the New York Central could not resolve their operating differences and philosophies to make the newly created Penn Central work. The two principals of the merger, Stuart Saunders of the Pennsylvania and Alfred Perlman of the New York Central, were as different as day is from night. The New York Central was basically a merchandising railroad, with innovative, unconventional management willing to try anything to improve the speed and quality of service (at least for freight). The Pennsylvania, on the other hand, was a highly conservative bureaucracy that contented itself with the volume service offered in steel, coal, and ore. Thus, the differences in these basic characteristics of the railroads and the men that directed them from the executive chairs was the first step that led to the eventual doom of the merged system.

The real test of fire came, however, in the actual operation of the Penn Central. The different operating rules, locomotive controls and signals, classification of cars, and routing of trains proved difficult enough for the pre-merger operating committees to reconcile, but they became a nightmare after the Penn Central started its actual operation. The merger had been proposed so that the two roads might eliminate thousands of miles of duplicating trackage and scores of surplus yards, at a total estimated annual savings of more than $80 million. In practice, this objective was never reached, because the operating railroaders stubbornly refused to adapt to the new practices and also because the local jurisdictions vigorously opposed any change in service as a result of the merger.

The computer systems serving each railroad were another visible symptom of the incompatibility of the two railroads. Not only were the computers themselves unable to form a unified data processing network, but the computer systems' personnel as well were as incompatible as the two railroads. The operation of the new railroad was beset by chaos. Cars were sent to the wrong destinations because New York Central personnel were unfamiliar with the routes of the Pennsylvania Railroad. Yardmasters sent entire trains out of their yards just to get rid of them. These trains found themselves abandoned on sidings because of the congestion in the yards. In one case near the end of 1968, a solid coal train was lost for two weeks outside of Syracuse. At many points on the system, taxicabs began to run a shuttle service to the trains, taking off crews that had worked their allotted twelve hours and bringing out fresh crews—which sometimes did nothing but continue to sit with their idled trains until some route opened up.

If the operations of the railroad were confusing and ill-directed, the operations of the corporate financial structure were even more bizarre. The Penn Central showed a profit on paper of some $90 million in 1968, while, in actuality, it had losses in excess of $20 million. The financial transactions involving the corporation's real estate holdings, investments, and subsidiary companies were baffling not only to the layman but to the financial analyst as well. By 1970, aggravated by a particularly severe winter, the losses incurred by the railroad began to show up to the point where the usual sources of capital—the investors and bondholders—were already viewing the Penn Central as a sinking ship. By then, the foundering railroad found itself unable to get any help from Washington; once-receptive Congressional and administration leaders now turned a deaf ear on the railroad's request for some $950 million in guaranteed loans. On June 9, 1970, Judge C. William Kraft signed the bankruptcy order for the largest railroad transportation company ever formed.

The Penn Central bankruptcy left shock waves within both the business community and the federal government. The stock market had already been headed downward for some time; suddenly a major corporation was bankrupt, and worse, the loss of a major railroad meant the possibility that automobiles, steel, coal, merchandise, and other commodities would not be able to move to their customers. Thus, not only was the railroad going under the waves, but it looked as if it might take many industries with it.

The trustees left with the job of running the railroad attempted to revive the bankrupt giant to some level of profitability, or at least to trim some of the losses, but it soon became evident that this was a more difficult proposition than putting Humpty Dumpty back together again. The old management's policy of deferred maintenance had left many miles of trackage in substandard condition. The locomotives and the rolling stock were scarcely in better shape. As a result, many hundreds of miles of track were subject to speed limits of ten miles per hour or less. Other lengths of trackage became the scenes of derailments, sometimes costing human lives. In one Indiana town, the derailment of several cars of liquid propane destroyed half the town. The property damage continued to mount. Unable to spend money to modernize its tracks, the railroad was caught in a squeeze: either spend money to fix the track, or spend money to pay damage claims.

Other factors also began to work against the railroad. Hurricane Agnes blew straight up through the Northeast, wiping out bridges and washing out roadbed to the point where repairs to these facilities ran into the multimillions of dollars. In the yards, scores of looters began to operate virtually unopposed in broad daylight, opening up trailer vans, boxcars, and refrigerator cars to pull colossal rip-offs and, again, making the claim payouts a staggering affair. Where the looters left off, the vandals began. Rocks and stones were hurled through caboose, locomotive, and commuter train windows. Bridges and buildings were defaced and sometimes burned or demolished. In some instances, derailments were caused by obstacles placed on the tracks or switches thrown open. Sometimes, human error, rather than vandalism, caused massive losses. In Cleveland, two 3000-horsepower diesel locomotives were instantly turned into scrap iron as a speeding freight slammed into an open drawbridge. In New York, a train running the wrong way through an open switch demolished six locomotives and hundreds of cars in one of the yards. Railroad service to the entire DelMarVa Peninsula was erased when a wayward barge wiped out the only railroad bridge leading from Maryland to the peninsula. The Poughkeepsie Bridge burned down, making it necessary for New England freight to go as far north as Albany before rolling into Massachusetts.

Perhaps the most bizarre incident that befell the troubled Penn Central was the apparent loss of a large number of boxcars that, months later, were discovered marked with the initials of another railroad—the LS&BC. Somehow, the car accountability system that served the Penn Central could not track these cars that had the PCRR symbols painted out and the LS&BC initials painted in; and, for all the world, it appeared as though there had actually been a theft of the Penn Central's cars. All of these symptoms indicated that the combination of the once-mighty New York Central and Pennsylvania railroads was on the road to nowhere. Faced with the discontinuance of railroad service to the most populated area of the country and still the most industrialized region of the world, the federal government at long last became involved. Hearings were held. Studies were conducted. The outlook was clear: the Penn Central could not make it on the road to recovery, and some form of massive intervention was needed. Some critics called for nationalization of the entire Northeast rail network. Others called for a complete dismemberment of the Penn Central, with the pieces to be absorbed by the profitable Chessie System, the Norfolk and Western, and even some of the southern and western railroads. The predominant view favored a federally supported corporation, which would absorb not only the Penn Central but other stricken railroads in the Northeast, such as the Erie-Lackawanna, the Lehigh Valley, and the Reading. In the meantime, the Penn Central's losses continued, and soon the day of reckoning loomed on the horizon. A shutdown became imminent when there was not enough money in the cash register to meet the payroll. Truly, the mighty Penn Central Railroad had indeed come to the verge of not only its own disaster, but also the economic disaster of much of the country. Help was desperately needed.

Under a late afternoon sun, a four-unit lashup heads east with a train of empty automobile racks at Brookpark, Ohio, a suburb of Cleveland. The lead unit is an ex–New York Central U-30B, part of a sizeable order of new locomotives that had been delivered just before the merger.

An eastbound merchandiser freight races through Conway Yards west of Pittsburgh during the last days of operation of the Pennsylvania Railroad. Although the Pennsy hauled steel and coal, it also carried a considerable fast-freight traffic, much of which duplicated the New York Central's efforts.

General Electric's Erie works was a big supplier of locomotives to the New York Central in the three years immediately preceding the PC merger. Similar locomotives were delivered to the Pennsylvania, all bearing the same numbers. Thus, one of the first premerger details was to renumber all cars and locomotives. Here, New York Central 2511 heads west through Rochester, N.Y., as a switching run sits in the adjacent yards. It would eventually be Penn Central 2511, and, still later, Conrail 2511.

The Pennsy main line east of Conway Yards was one of the most heavily travelled sections of railway found anywhere in the country. In addition to a steady procession of freights into the yards, there were scores of symbol freights bypassing the yards on the outside tracks. Here, 6502 leads a trio of General Electric–built locomotives with a solid consist of empty automobile racks. A second westbound freight is moving up on the lead track into the yards, while an eastbound freight that has already cleared the yards can be seen in the distance.

In snow-gripped Cleveland, a two-unit EMD F-7 consist prepares to head west with a transfer freight from Collinwood Yards to the west side of the city. These General Motors–built locomotives were the replacements for the magnificent fleet of steam locomotives that once served the Water Level Route. As part of New York Central's simplification of maintenance, the classic gray-and-black paint job was replaced with solid black, with white stripes and letters. These would be the principal colors of the new Penn Central.

The Pennsylvania ran multitudes of branch lines throughout nearly all of its system. Some were important connector lines; others served only small localities. All of them demanded service. Here, a three-unit Alco RS-3 combo lays down an oil smoke trail with a string of empty hopper cars on the line to New Castle, Pa.

The merger may have developed all at once, but one of the most visible signs of merger—the appearance of New York Central equipment on Pennsylvania Railroad trackage—did not take place immediately. The biggest reason was the different features each railroad had installed aboard their locomotives. The Pennsylvania had automatic cab signals located at the controls of each unit; the New York Central did not. The Central, on the other hand, had automatic train control features on its locomotives, which

The merger of the two railroads was already six months old when this photo of eastbound and westbound freights was taken near Ambridge, Pa. Pennsy railroaders were already growling over the confusion taking place with their runs, the long times spent waiting out on the main line, and the fact that the Pennsy was now something else again. Soon, the red keystone would be replaced once and for good by the interlocked P and C, the symbol of the new road.

prevented a train from entering a block that was occupied by another train. Thus, if different locomotives did show up on the other railroad, they were always used as trailing units, never as lead units. Repainting to the Penn Central color scheme also did not occur very rapidly.

While the Pennsylvania Railroad emerged from the merger as the major corporate entity, the operating characteristics of the Penn Central were clearly those of the New York Central. The century-green color scheme that the Central used on all its cars and cabooses was adopted as the color scheme of the Penn Central. Locomotives were to be black with white trim and numerals, just like those on the Central. The only trace of Pennsy identity was in the high eight-inch cab numerals. Renumbering of all equipment began even before the merger, with little difficulty. It was to be one of the few instances where the merger would be brought about smoothly.

It was only a matter of time before the New York Central's locomotives would be found deep inside Pennsy territory. Here, a NYC GP-35 follows a pair of heavy Pennsy six-axle SD-45s into the approaches to Conway Yards. It has already been renumbered to the 2300-series used by the Pennsy's similar-class locomotives. The New York Central never needed heavy six-axle power, but soon these locomotives were turning up in places such as Boston, Syracuse, Buffalo, and other points along the Water Level Route.

To the rail fan, the merger of the two railroads represented some interesting days. There was the anticipation of seeing different locomotives on rails that had only known one type in years upon years of operation. There were the long freights that seemed to parade by endlessly, making the Penn Central look like the busiest railroad in the world. How were we to know that these were goods and merchandise trains trying to find their destinations after constant rerouting?

It was hard to realize that at one time these two railroads had been the bitterest of rivals, with their crack passenger trains racing against each other and the clock. The keystone of the Pennsy and the oval emblem of the New York Central seemed to be the very symbols of the most intense competition in the world. And here they were, first side by side and soon vanishing as the "friendly worms" trademark of the new Penn Central began to appear everywhere. It was truly the end of an era, and the beginning of another chapter in American railroading.

Sitting side by side in the Conway, Pennsylvania locomotive terminal are New York Central's 1706 and two Pennsy heavy-duty six-axle units.

The 6180 was originally designed to haul freights over the Alleghenies. But here it sits at the head of a southbound freight in the PC's Moraine Yards at Dayton, Ohio, which was formerly New York Central territory. One of the early NYC F-7 locomotives can be seen as the third unit in this lashup.

6180

Soon, the PC emblem could be seen everywhere. At top, a string of empties heads westbound out of Enola Yards near Harrisburg, Pa. At bottom, two GG-1s roll a freight past Crystal City in Arlington, Va. and into Potomac Yards. At top right, a switching crew is at work in Moraine, Ohio, while, at bottom right, a two-unit SD-45 combination hauls a trailer-train hotshot along ex-Pennsy trackage in Dayton, Ohio.

PACIFIC
FRUIT
EXPRESS
9014

6136
6136

The River Division of the Penn Central was one of the most heavily trafficked sections of the entire railroad, forming a link from PC's Perlman Yard at Selkirk, N.Y., through New Jersey and on into Potomac Yard. It also was the scene of constant derailments and delays, as the overworked single-track line saw a constant procession of freights. Here, two GP-38s and a GP-40 proceed with a southbound trailer train, with the Bear Mountain Bridge in the background. ***(Photo by John Taibi)***

8060
8048
PENN CENTRAL
8048

Ohio was another sector of the PC where the rails were never quiet for very long. In much of this part of the system, deteriorating roadbed caused speed limits of ten miles per hour to be put into effect. At upper left, an eastbound freight rolls over the Miami River bridge at Dayton, Ohio. Lower left, ex-NYC units 3078 and 2825 (still in its NYC paint job) head east to Springfield, Ohio. Top right, four "covered wagons" haul a westbound freight through Brookpark, Ohio, while, in the lower right, a pair of SD-40s roll past Cleveland Memorial Stadium on a westbound run.

The top photograph shows the workhorse of the entire system—the SD-45. The Pennsy ordered this locomotive, EMD's most powerful unit, to haul freight over the Allegheny mountains, but the PC soon used it everywhere on the system. In ex-Central territory, it was used extensively in freight service over the Berkshires, and it could also be used on the flat stretches of track as well. The six-axle units were among the heaviest locomotives in use, and, together with the mammoth new freight cars travelling at high speeds, they began to wear down the roadbed. The side photo shows an ex-NYC GP-9 switching at Brookpark Yard in Cleveland. These GP-9s were at one time used exclusively for fast freight and Flexi-Van service, but, after the merger, they were relegated to yard duties.

PENN CENTRAL
7452
12758

Two diesel units—one built by General Electric, the other by General Motors EMD Division—haul a solitary caboose westward through the north side of Pittsburgh. The merger was two years old at the time this photograph was taken, yet the old color schemes of the Pennsy are evident in the trailing locomotive unit and the caboose.

2635 2635
CENTRAL
2635

In the Washington-to-New York corridor of the Pennsy, the electrified portion of the line also saw the conversion to the Penn Central. GG-1s, which were the very symbol of the Pennsy, soon took on the PC lettering of the merged road. Even the Metroliner, which represented the Pennsy's most aggressive venture into high-speed passenger service, was now a Penn Central trademark. The old Pennsy had even ordered new electric locomotives to haul volume freight between New York City and Potomac Yards. Shown here is the *Southern Crescent* on its way to New York through Landover, Md. At top right, the *Metroliner* is also New York bound, pictured at Landover. The bottom right photograph shows two EH-44 electric units with a Potomac Yards—bound freight. Some of these units never received the PC paint scheme, an indication that, by 1973, the Penn Central had stopped all unnecessary maintenance of locomotives and cars.

CENTRAL
2235

3206

By 1973, the Penn Central was in receivership, but, from a trackside camera's view, the trains still continued to roll. At left, a diesel unit rolls northward with a freight out of Potomac Yards in Alexandria, Va., evidently headed for non-electrified territory and thus not requiring a locomotive change. Bottom left, a PC and four Southern Railway run-through locomotives haul a southbound trailer train across the Miami River in Dayton, Ohio. Below, an eastbound TV symbol freight moves along at a snail's pace with the skyline of Dayton in the background. The New York Central's idea of using containers on flat cars for merchandise freight had given way to the Pennsy's truck-train concept. The deteriorating roadbed had reduced these fast freights to speeds slower than switching locals in many places.

In the early 1970s, when the merger of the railroads was being attacked by business analysts, railroad transportation specialists, the general public, and especially those who had opposed the merger in the first place, one could visit many places on the railroad and still see the individual character of the two railroads that had formed this colossal failure. In the hills of Pennsylvania, the ore and coal trains rolled just as they had during the days of the Pennsy. It was unthinkable that railroad service would ever stop. Such a shutdown would close down the mines, stop the mills, and paralyze everything else. Along the Water Level Route of the Central, hundreds upon hundreds of businesses depended upon the railroad to bring in their raw materials and haul away the finished products to market. True, the colors had changed, but in many cases the equipment was still the same, and the railroad was, to many, still the Pennsy or the Central. But, in those days of 1973, 1974, and 1975, many people listened to the news anxiously, because when the day came that the railroad could not meet its payroll, that would be the day that the rails would once and for all be stilled.

At bottom left, John Taibi has photographed an ore and coal train rolling through the hills of central Pennsylvania behind two locomotives already showing the signs of wear and tear, and no repair. These locomotives would be operated without maintenance until repairs became prohibitive. At that point, they would be cannibalized for spare parts. At top, some old New York Central veterans in new PC color schemes haul a local freight eastbound through Brookpark, Ohio. These locomotives also would be retired or traded in rather than repaired.

For high-volume shippers such as power utilities, the railroad represented lifeblood itself, and any slowdown or shutdown of service would be catastrophic, especially when the business was that of supplying power and light to the city of Detroit. Detroit Edison inaugurated a unit train service that would use Penn Central trackage, but would consist of its own equipment. To do this, Detroit Edison ordered a fleet of locomotives and a vast number of coal hopper cars that could be rapidly unloaded over rotary dumpers at the power plant. The famous four-track Air Line which the New York Central had built through Toledo had now been chopped down to three tracks. Two of the tracks were used for Penn Central traffic and active Detroit Edison trains. The third track was a transport and storage line for Detroit Edison trains. Solid unit trains could be seen sitting on these tracks for days at a time. The locomotives would be idling and locked up, many times without anybody around them at all. Thus, to this one shipper, the Penn Central was literally a pipeline on wheels, with Detroit Edison supplying the motion to this pipeline.

An eastbound and a westbound freight meet on the west side of the Miami River bridge in Dayton, Ohio.

A pair of silver-and-blue Detroit Edison SD-40s with a PC SD-40 thrown in for good measure roll by the deserted Toledo Union Terminal. At one time, this newest of railroad stations was the crew change and inspection point for every one of the New York Central's crack passenger trains. The terminal now sits lifeless as this new type of railroading takes over. At bottom, two more Detroit Edison locomotives sit idling with a unit train, waiting for the supply schedules to send them rolling towards one of the DE power stations with a trainload of energy. ***(Both photos by Howard Ameling)***

PENN CENTRAL
4859
PENN CENTRAL

The inveterate GG-1 continued to move heavy freights through the electrified territory despite age and changes in freights consists and ownership. At top left, two units roll northbound through Washington, D.C., with a freight out of Potomac Yards. Below, an eastbound merchandise freight rolls out of the Indianapolis branch and onto the joint PC-B&O line that ran through the center of Dayton, Ohio.

3102
PENN CENTRAL
3156

In the merged Penn Central system, there were two ways of carrying trailer van freight. One way was to carry the trailer including its wheels on a flat car. The other way, called Flexi-Van, used a specially-built flat car to haul just the container. The Flexi-Van concept developed by the New York Central lost out. It was used solely for mail and express runs. When the U.S. Postal Service began to use the airlines almost exclusively to haul mail, Flexi-Van disappeared from the Penn Central. Here an eastbound mail and express rolls through Dayton, Ohio, bound for Springfield and, eventually, Cleveland.

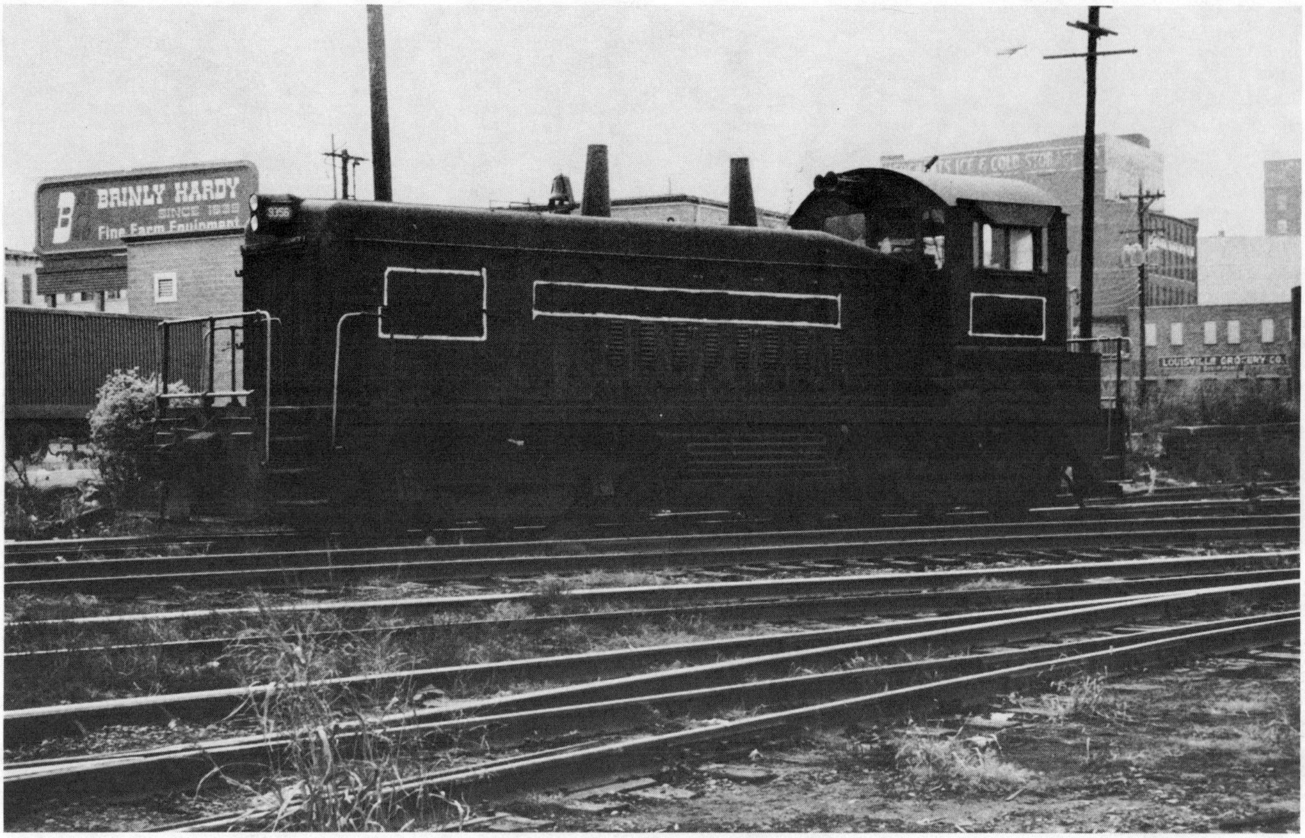
BRINLY HARDY
Fine Farm Equipment
LOUISVILLE GROCERY CO.

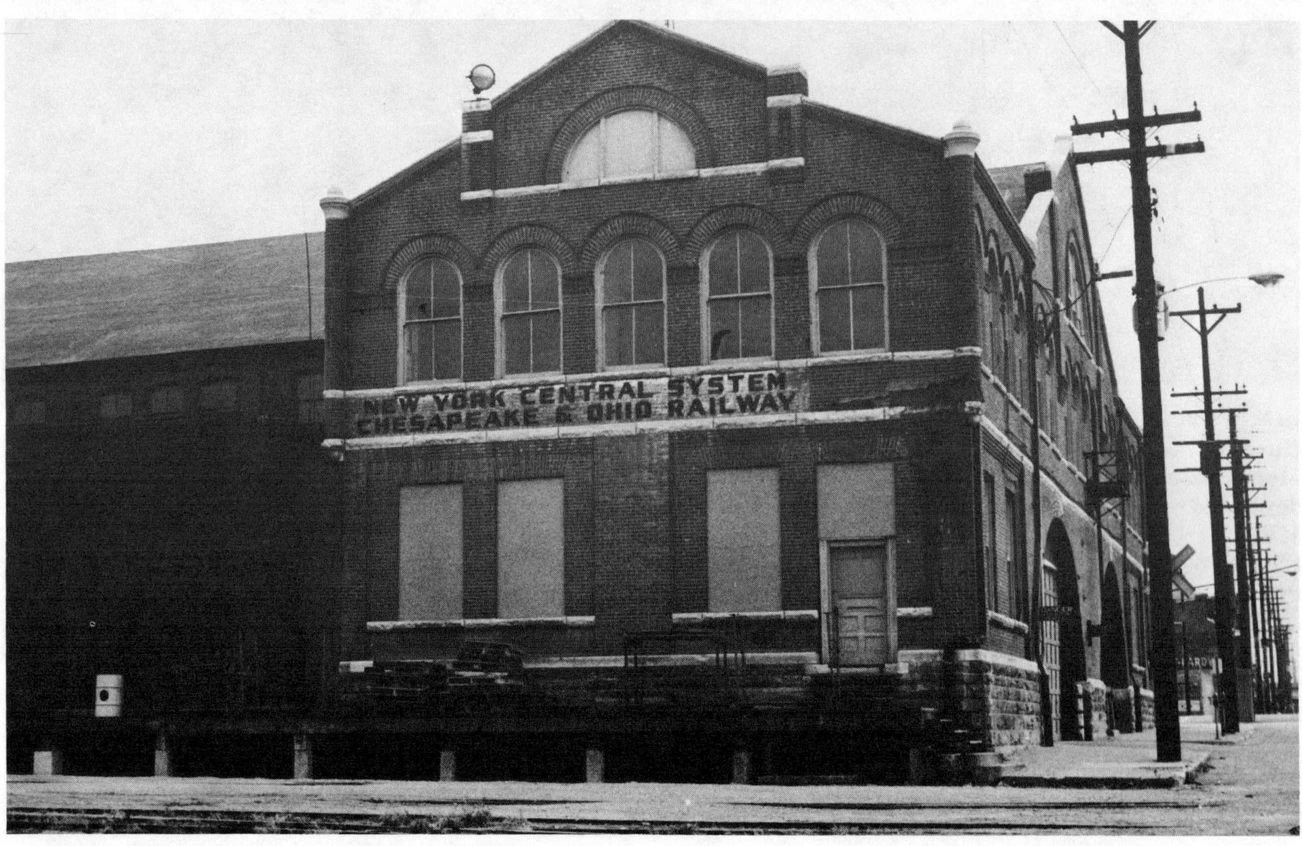

NEW YORK CENTRAL SYSTEM
CHESAPEAKE & OHIO RAILWAY

An abandoned roundhouse at Jeffersonville, Ind.

By 1974, the ravages of wear, bankruptcy, and near-insolvency were appearing everywhere on the system. The camera of Leonard Dunman has portrayed some of the visual symptoms of the system's decay in the Louisville area. At top, a switcher sits on a siding with all its lettering and numerals painted out. The middle photograph shows what used to be the freight terminal that served both the New York Central and the Chesapeake and Ohio.

At one time, the 7403 was one of the many GP-9s that hauled the fast freight along the New York Central's Big Four routes. It was photographed by Leonard Dunman sitting at the Clarksville, Ind., enginehouse, with characteristic faded numerals and an appearance saying that it has been many months since it last saw the inside of a maintenance shop. At right is the Big Four bridge from Louisville to Jeffersonville, literally going nowhere. Local pressure forced the approaches to be torn down, but neither the bankrupt Penn Central nor any other organization would pay for the demolition of the main span across the Ohio River. ***(Both photos by Leonard Dunman.)***

As if things were not bad enough for the embattled Penn Central, the floods and winds of Hurricane Agnes that blew into the Northeast in June 1972 made a shambles of bridges, track, and everything else resembling railroad property. With meager resources to keep operations rolling even in the good times, the Penn Central now found itself in the position of having to repair whole sections of track and many bridges that had been washed out by the floods that ravaged the area. For about one year, many sections of track were not able to be restored to service. The effects of Hurricane Agnes, added to the rest of the problems facing the Penn Central and other railroads in the Northeast, made the future of these railroads certain of one thing: they could not continue to exist in their present form. Some sort of reorganization was needed, and needed quickly, for otherwise these rails would be quiet—for a long time to come.

The Chemung River Bridge of the Corning Branch, a link between the lines of upper Pennsylvania and New York State, lies partially submerged in the river after flood waters washed out the bridge.

The Susquehanna River Bridge at Selinsgrove, Pa., sits with flood debris piled through the superstructure and onto the tracks.

Roadbed washouts occurred at many points along the Penn Central. One of the most complete demolitions of roadbed is pictured on the Elmira Branch, where the ballast has been completely removed, leaving the rails and the crossties suspended in mid-air. ***(All photos on these pages are courtesy of the Penn Central.)***

Despite the economic collapse of the Penn Central, the operating foul-ups, and the threat of complete shutdowns, the railroad will still remain in the memories of the railfan. At no portion of the Penn Central were the tracks ever lacking for activity for very long, be it in the many lines through the Midwest, or along the shores of the Great Lakes, or through the hills of Pennsylvania, or along the electrified portion of the line from Washington to New York. Although at a snail's pace due to bad roadbed or undermaintained locomotives, the trains still managed to roll.

The sight of powerful black road units with their white "friendly worms" PC logo was still something to watch from the side of the tracks. It was overpowering to hear the sound of this power heading towards you with all that tonnage, even though the trains would operate so slowly at times that you could read the destination labels written on the sides of the cars. Many times, trains would stop for a horizontal signal (Pennsy) or a red block (Central), and you would have a chance to visit with the crew and hear their views on where this railroad was headed.

While railroaders were reassured by both unions and management that they would have a job, there was always the doubt. But they still ran the trains, despite all.

Towards the last days of the Penn Central's operation, there were still portions of the system where train-watching was an exciting experience. At Newport, Pa., on the ex-Pennsy main line, a westbound Enola-to-Conway freight passes by with a mixture of locomotives representing twenty years of locomotive building. ***(Photo by John Taibi.)***

3089

Out on the west end of Cleveland, another westbound freight gets under way in late afternoon. Above, a north-bound freight rolls through Lanham, Md., behind a pair of EH-44 electric motors.

2

The Successful Roads: Chessie and Norfolk and Western

While the Penn Central was settling into bankruptcy and possible dismemberment, other railroads, some operating in or close to the territory of the Penn Central, were showing healthy records for earnings and profits. Two railroads stood out in stark comparison to the operations of the Penn Central. These were the Chessie System and the Norfolk and Western.

It was ironic that both of these railroads were themselves merged railways. The Chessie was the product of the merger of the Baltimore and Ohio and the Chesapeake and Ohio railroads, with the later addition of the Western Maryland Railroad. The Norfolk and Western was the product of the original Norfolk and Western, the Nickel Plate Road, and the Wabash. Undoubtedly, both of these mergers caused operating problems when they first developed, but in neither case did these operating problems strangle the system.

Several factors helped the formation of both of these systems. The Chessie merger was not so much a corporate consolidation as a working cooperative relationship between the participating railroads. Only through a gradual process of consolidation and increasing these working arrangements did the Chessie System begin to evolve as a single railroad. The distinctive "sleeping cat" logo and yellow, orange, and blue color scheme of the railroad still show the identity of the three participating railroads. To many, the B&O still is the B&O, and the C&O still has its own identity. Only the Western Maryland seems to have been totally assimilated by the Chessie System. In the case of the Norfolk and Western, the merger was an end-to-end merger rather than an overlapping and consolidation merger. The original N&W did not run in the territory of either the Nickel Plate or the Wabash, and the other two railroads also had little overlap. Thus, one large railroad emerged out of three smaller lines.

Coal was the mainstay of both railroads. Both railroads hauled a considerable volume of coal traffic, which decreased only when there was a coal strike or a steel strike. Much of this coal traffic was for export, and was transported from the mines eastward to the ports of Baltimore, Norfolk, and Portsmouth. The B&O served not only an east-west market but a south-north market as well, with lines running from Pennsylvania and Ohio to every one of the major Great Lakes ports. The Wabash and the Nickel Plate were both merchandise-hauling roads, thus complementing the Norfolk and Western's coal traffic with additional commodity markets.

One of the newest locomotives to be placed in service on the Chessie Systems roars through Point of Rocks, Md., with a solid string of empty hopper cars headed westward for the mines of Western Pennsylvania and Ohio. On its side are the initials "WM," indicative of the fact that, although the Chessie System is the parent road, this is a Western Maryland locomotive. Above right, an EMD F-7, one of the oldest locomotives on the Chessie System, gets ready to start its northbound run out of Potomac Yard. Below, B&O 3743 heads eastbound through Dayton, Ohio, on the B&O's Cincinnati-Toledo line.

The Nickel Plate, in particular, had given the New York Central extremely vigorous competition in the Chicago-to-Buffalo marketing territory. The Baltimore and Ohio and the Pennsylvania Railroad had historically been competitive railroads. Thus, both Chessie and Norfolk and Western were active competitors within Penn Central territory, and managed to siphon off a significant amount of traffic when the Penn Central was gripped by shipper delays in freight traffic. Moreover, when the railroad reorganization plans were unfolded by the planners and the legislators, some plan versions had the Chessie and the Norfolk and Western taking on huge chunks of the dismembered Penn Central and five other bankrupt roads.

From a trainwatcher's observation, there was indeed an enormous difference in watching the Penn Central limp along while Chessie raced hotshot merchandiser freights along the two-track main line through suburban Maryland. Another measure of success was the solid mile-long coal trains rolling constantly along the rails leading to the Tidewater ports of Virginia. On one hand was a bankrupt rail system still losing money whichever way it turned; on the other hand were two rail systems that not only were profitable among transportation companies—they were just plain profitable amongst any type of industry.

A Baltimore and Ohio switching run winds along an embankment in Dayton, Ohio, headed northward for the yards in the northern part of the city. Above, the B&O takes control of the Penn Central-B&O joint trackage in the middle of Dayton. A northbound freight headed by two GP-40s passes a southbound freight containing a solid consist of automobiles.

Three C&O units head north into Potomac Yards through Alexandria Va. Of all the railroads using Potomac Yards, only the Chessie System operates out of both ends of the yards. All southbound trains are clearly C&O, while the B&O operates out of the north portion of the yards. Yet, motive power in exchanged constantly.

Comparatively speaking, a train watcher could stand around a section of B&O main line and wait for hours before anything showed up, whereas, on the Penn Central, the frequency of trains made railfan activity more interesting. However, there were those times of day when the B&O operated just as frequently along many portions of its system. Dayton was the scene of heavy B&O activity as traffic moved between Cincinnati and Detroit with automobiles, steel, chemicals, and, above all, coal. Potomac Yards was another area where B&O activity was heavy. The blue and yellow locomotives ran constantly, all over the system, and one could see the steady modernization of both motive power and roadbed.

The B&O rolls through some of the most scenic areas of the Northeast, and the bridge crossing over the Potomac at Harper's Ferry, W. Va., is one of the outstanding portions of the entire line. Here, John Taibi found a spot high over the cliffs overlooking the bridge and the town, and caught this eastbound coal train headed for Brunswick, Md., and ultimately, the port of Baltimore.

A northbound train carrying solid empty automobile-rack cars heads down a stretch of track in Dayton. Within another mile, the B&O trackage divides from the Penn Central lines that this train is currently using. At lower left, a westbound B&O freight eases out of the B&O line and onto the PC line through the center of Dayton. Below, a northbound B&O freight heads out of Potomac Yards for its run to Baltimore, headed by C&O 7506. The consolidation of the B&O with the C&O resulted in the sharing of equipment and facilities, with each railroad still maintaining its own separate identity.

Another B&O freight rolls westward out of the B&O trackage at Dayton, this time in late afternoon. Unlike some railroads, which restrict certain types of locomotives to given territories of the system, the B&O uses its motive power anywhere and everywhere. In addition, locomotives of the C&O would also turn up regularly. At top right, another eastbound freight heads through Dayton with tri-level automobile racks. Note the metallic shields on the sides of these cars, made necessary to stop vandals from throwing rocks through the windows of automobiles in transit. At lower right, a commuter run says good-night to homeward-bound passengers in Gaithersburg, Md. At one time, these Budd RDC cars were the famed *Speedliners* that the B&O thought would hypo its Philadelphia to Washington passenger service. Today they are used in suburban Washington commuter service, and can be immediately identified by the black exhaust smokescreen, which would make any steam locomotive look good by comparison.

B&O

3581 3581
B&O

1977
B&O
1977
Chessie System
6953

GM50 GM50
B&O
Chessie System

Top left, the 1977 sits at the head end of a southbound freight at Willard, Ohio. Below left, the solid gold GM50 does a bit of local freight switching around Deshler, Ohio. Above, the Chessie System has now been increased by the addition of the Western Maryland, where a WM F-7 looks across at a brand-new EMD GP-40 4246. Until Conrail ordered fifty more EMD GP-40s, the Chessie System had the largest number of these locomotives of any American railroad system. ***(All photos on these pages by Howard Ameling)***

In the fall of 1972, the Chessie System unveiled its new image, a brilliant yellow-orange-blue color scheme with a sleeping-cat "C" as its logo. The sleeping cat, nicknamed "Chessie," had long been the symbol of the Chesapeake and Ohio Railroad, and appeared in advertisments for its passenger service. The B&O-C&O system thus took on its official name of Chessie System. However, the separate identity of each railroad was retained in all equipment, even though the Chessie now was using a common numbering system. Along with this new image was a new order for one of the largest fleets of four-axle, 3000-horsepower locomotives in history—the EMD GP-40.

This was also the occasion of the 150th anniversary of the B&O, and, in addition, the 50th anniversary of the Electro-Motive Division (EMD) of General Motors. To commemorate this, the B&O unveiled the Chessie new image with a locomotive numbered 1977, and EMD delivered to the B&O a solid-gold-painted unit numbered GM50. Eventually, both locomotives would be renumbered, and the GM50 would be repainted in the new Chessie colors. However, the gold unit was still to be seen in its commemorative colors as late as the summer of 1978. It represented yet another historical milestone in American railroading.

WESTERN MARYLAND
7495
WESTERN MARYLAND

At left, a Western Maryland pusher hauls the last of AJ-1, a Norfolk and Western run-through, over a fifteen-mile grade on the Western Maryland route. John Taibi describes this portion of the Western Maryland as having been taken out of service since the WM joined the Chessie System. This line, at Corriganville, Md., now lies virtually quiet, with all of the traffic now being routed over the B&O line between Cumberland, Md., and Connellsville, Pa. At top, a C&O SD-40 teams with a late-model B&O GP-40 on a westbound late-afternoon run through Gaithersburg, Md. At bottom, the B&O is pictured on the joint Penn Central–B&O trackage in Southwest Washington, D.C., on a northbound trip. Many government buildings can be seen in the background.

John Taibi caught this shot of a westbound Chessie freight on the B&O main line at Lowellsville, Ohio, behind two repainted B&O GP-40s, 3717 and 3724. Like most large mergers, the creation of the Chessie System resulted in a mixture of color schemes on locomotives and cars, representing the former railroads of an earlier era in management. At left, a trio of GP-40s blasts over the Potomac River bridge at Harper's Ferry, W. Va., with a solid consist of coal. Above, a pair of old-timer F-7s of the Western Maryland races west with a Martinsburg (W.Va.) turnaround. Although the Western Maryland still exists as a railroad entity, much of its operation has been rerouted over the B&O lines, and the result has been a mixture of B&O blue, Chessie yellow, C&O blue, and Western Maryland's two different color schemes. This did not, however, begin to approach the wild assortment of locomotives that were later brought together in the formation of Conrail.

The improvements still continue on the Chessie. Even more and newer locomotives are still joining the fleet of power that operates on the system. In the period from 1975 through 1980, the Chessie System had ordered over 400 additional GP40-2 locomotives from EMD as well as over 100 new B30-7 locomotives from General Electric. The roadbed is now receiving continuous welded rail, which will further speed up the thundering freights on this line and reduce the amount of derailments due to bad roadbed.

Perhaps the best place to see the Chessie System in operation is in the Point of Rocks–Brunswick–Harper's Ferry area. The scenery provides a suitable backdrop to the many kinds of rail activity taking place there. Heavy coal trains blast along the bridge over the Potomac at Harper's Ferry, stop in the Brunswick yards momentarily to change crews, then continue over the Old Line to Sykesville and Baltimore. Fast trailer-train freights head down the line to Silver Spring and Washington, there to swing south to Potomac Yards in Alexandria or else to sweep north to Baltimore. The silver fleet of commuter trains comes alive at Brunswick in the morning and returns home to end the day by nightfall. The fascination of railroading has attracted many railfans to this area, from the days of steam right up to the present. It probably will attract railfans for many years to come.

Even though the Chessie System was a substantial competitor of the Penn Central and, later, the Conrail network, the two railroads participated in run-through agreements in which motive power was interchanged, sometimes at locations where none of the participating railroads had ever operated before. This scene is at Rutherford Yards in Harrisburg, Pa., which once upon a time was owned by the Reading Railroad. At the left is an ex-Pennsylvania Railroad GP-30, now relegated by its new owner to switching duties. At right, a Chessie run-through from Hagerstown enters the yards eastbound on the termination of its run. Sometimes this freight uses mixed Conrail and Chessie power, and at other times it can be seen with power belonging to either railway.

At left, an early morning hotshot freight roars westward past the old Rockville passenger station, which now serves only the two-a-day Amtrak arrivals and all of the Washington commuter trade. Below left, another eastbound coal train pounds over the bridge at Harper's Ferry. The tower operator in the station in the background claims that this bridge sees more rail fan tourists in the course of a year than any other point on the B&O. Since Harper's Ferry itself is a historical landmark, it is easy to see why this is so.

Below, three new GP-40s sandwich in an old Western Maryland F7 "B" unit on a westbound run of empty coal cars headed through Point of Rocks, Md.

The camera of Howard Ameling has recorded the transition of the old Nickel Plate Road into the new Norfolk and Western. Above, a local unit crosses the Sandusky River at Fremont, Ohio. Below, two ex-Wabash F-7s roar westward with icicles hanging from their sides at Conneaut, Ohio, in the teeth of the winter of 1977. Above right, another freight, this one consisting of GP-9s from all of N&W's predecessor roads, grinds westward through Bellevue, Ohio.

The first of the large-scale mergers, preceding that of the Penn Central, was the creation of the new Norfolk and Western from five other rail systems. This merger occurred in several stages. The first stage, which took place in the late 1950s, was the Norfolk and Western's acquisition of the coal-hauling Virginian Railroad. In the next step, the Nickel Plate Road acquired trackage rights through the Pittsburgh and West Virginia Railroad, thus extending the NKP down into the steel country from its original acquisition of the Wheeling and Lake Erie. The final and largest phase of the N&W merger was the consolidation of the N&W with the Nickel Plate Road and the Wabash Railroad. This created a railroad giant which extended from southern Virginia and Kentucky northward to the Great Lakes, and from Norfolk westward all the way to Omaha, Nebr. The Norfolk and Western, once a coal-hauling road, now handled a diversified mix of freight, and became an awesome competitor for other northeastern roads because it could haul freight from the West straight through to the eastern markets without passing through the Chicago gateway.

The new Norfolk and Western also provided rail fans with some unusual sights at its scenes of operations. Above left, two ex–Nickel Plate units get ready to depart Bellevue, Ohio, on a westbound run. One is still in NKP colors while the other has already been transformed into a N&W unit. At lower left, another NKP freight eases out of the Bellevue yards, this one renumbered to the N&W roster but still sporting its old colors. An old Fairbanks-Morse switcher stands on the adjacent track. Below, the repainting program to convert all locomotives to the N&W color scheme apparently had taken place so hurriedly that the paint job didn't take—as shown by this Fairbanks-Morse Train-Master unit, with half of it still showing its Wabash colors and the bottom half of it painted Norfolk and Western. All Fairbanks-Morse units have since been retired. ***(All photos courtesy of Howard Ameling)***

1307
NW
1307
ACFX
53742

Like all railroads in the northeast, the N&W also had to brave the heat of summer and the cold blasts of winter. On a hot summer day, a westbound N&W freight hurries by the Cleveland Rapid Transit line in the western part of the city. At top, Howard Ameling braved a typical Northern Ohio blizzard to capture this eastbound N&W freight getting under way in the N&W yards at Bellevue.

Because the Norfolk and Western now stretched all the way to Omaha on its northwestern route, and ran into St. Louis on its southwestern leg, it was only natural that it would soon find run-through partners with the western roads. Thus, N&W trains began to operate into places like Denver and on west into California. In return, the Union Pacific and the Southern Pacific sent their motive power on east. Thus, the trainwatcher saw portions of Ohio looking like scenes out west, with many, many Union Pacific locomotives all clustered together on any number of trains. The Southern Pacific SD-45-T units, traditionally the power seen on the mountain ranges of California and specially equipped to operate through long tunnels, now were seen even on local freights in Ohio.

At top, *five* (count 'em!) UP units and two dead N&W units start out westbound on a freight out of Bellevue, Ohio, caught by the lens of Howard Ameling. Below, Ed Durnwald photographed this eastbound N&W trailer-train leaving Conneaut, Ohio, on its way to Buffalo, the farthest east any Union Pacific locomotive would go on N&W trackage. *(Photo from the collection of Howard Ameling)* At right, a cold day in December sees wall-to-wall Union Pacific power tied up in Bellevue, Ohio, as a grain train and a coal train sit side by side. A scene like this would be typical in the vast stretches of the west served by the Union Pacific, but hardly expected in an Ohio railroad town.

UNION PACIFIC
UNION PACIFIC
We can handle it.
2895

Two Southern Pacific SD-45T-2s and a U-36C lead two other N&W units out of Bellevue, Ohio, with a westbounder. The "T" designator of the SD-45s is unique to the Southern Pacific and the Rio Grande. Because of the long tunnels in the California mountain ranges, air must be scooped in close to the tracks rather than in the usual top location in these diesel units; the heavy hot-exhaust buildup in the tunnels cannot provide the necessary cool air for these locomotives. Nonetheless, even these locomotives found their way east in run-through service.

An SP six-axle U-36C leads three N&W units on a freight westbound for the Lima Division at Bellevue, Ohio.

A Cotton Belt (subsidiary of the SP) SD-45 heads a local over the B&O trackage at Deshler, Ohio. Besides operating all over the N&W, Southern Pacific run-through power is frequently used on the Chessie System in Ohio and has turned up in other places on the B&O as well. The Penn Central, Conrail, and especially the Seaboard Coast Line have had the red and gray of the SP system on their property. *(All photos courtesy of Howard Ameling)*

After getting a clear block signal, this four-unit coal train is getting under way at Payne, Ohio, headed for Indiana. While the Norfolk and Western is characterized as a coal-hauling railroad, its Nickel Plate Road merger created even additional coal traffic, from southeastern Ohio to the Great Lakes. *(Photo courtesy of Howard Ameling)*

The Norfolk and Western was not a big subscriber to the low-nose profile. All new power was like the 1905 majority of other railroads ordered, although many of the locomotives acquired through the merger had the low nose profile. All new power was like the 1905 pictured above, with cab visibility available through the narrow side window. *(Photo taken at Bellevue, Ohio, by Howard Ameling)* Opposite, the camera of Tom Hildreth captures two N&W run-through freights in the dead of winter at East Worcester, NY, on Delaware and Hudson trackage. The N&W run-through agreements with the D&H and the Boston and Maine, and here freights NE-84 and NE-87 meet.

Amtrak's new French TurboTrain

The United Aircraft TurboTrain.

The Turboliner—equipped *Salt City Express*

The *Blue Ridge* at Harper's Ferry W. Va.

Four U-36 Bs, originally intended for Auto-Train, now painted in Conrail blue

An Enola-bound freight on the Susquehanna River Bridge

A westbound freight on the Hackensack River Bridge

A mixed E-L and RDG lashup at Arden N.Y.

The Southern Pacific comes to Conrail

A three-unit Erie-Lackawanna consist heads a westbound freight through Port Jervis, N.Y.

A Conrail trailer-train at Bear Mountain, N.Y.

Conrail's Bicentennial Express at Sufferin, N.Y. on July 4, 1976

The Erie-Lackawanna Bicentennial units and the Delaware and Hudson 1776 at Starucca Viaduct in New York.

A second Delaware and Hudson Bicentennial locomotive

A Conrail GG-1 in Bicentennial colors

The New York, Ontario and Western in red, white and blue

The Pittsburg and Lake Erie in red and white stripes

The Reading 4-8-4 2102 pulled the Freedom Train

Its sister locomotive, 2101 was painted in Chessie colors and sent out on fan trips

Conrail's 4935 back in Pennsylvania Railroad colors

SOUTHERN
PACIFIC
NW

As the 1980's commenced, both railroads—the Chessie System and the Norfolk and Western—announced plans for expansion through further mergers. The Chessie System and the Family Lines, consisting of the Seaboard Coast Line, the Louisville and Nashville, the Clinchfield Railroad, and the Atlanta and West Point Line, announced merger plans to create the CSX Corporation. This would represent a new rail network almost as vast as Conrail's, extending from the Great Lakes to the Gulf of Mexico, and from the Mississippi to every port city on the Atlantic Coast except Boston.

Not to be outdone, the Norfolk and Western found a merger partner of its own, the vast and profitable Southern Railway, and in mid-1980, announced plans for the merger. This would create a single railway network throughout the Midwest, the Northeast, and the Southeast, making the entire Eastern Section of the country dominated by three principal railroads—CSX, the N&W/Southern System, and Conrail.

NORFOLK AND WESTERN
ZIM

3
The Passenger Railroads: Amtrak and Auto-Train

By the late 1960s, it had become inescapably clear that the railroad passenger train was headed for extinction. Because the railroads had seen fit to downgrade this service to the point where only a masochist would dare ride the trains, and because the private automobile and the jet had lured vast numbers of the travelling public away from rail travel, passenger trains were now virtually empty. The railroads could not get rid of their passenger service fast enough. The only area of the country where passenger train travel amounted to anything at all was the Northeast Corridor, where the Pennsylvania Railroad operated frequent service between Washington and New York. It, too, was nothing to rave about, with the exception of the experimental *Metroliner,* which held forth a new promise of extremely comfortable seats and the fastest passenger train schedules in the country. Alarmed that passenger train travel would indeed die out, Congress passed the Rail Passenger Service Act of 1970, which provided for the designation of a basic national rail passenger system and the creation of a National Railroad Passenger Corporation. Its charter called for it to provide intercity rail passenger service, employing innovative operating and marketing concepts so as to develop fully the potential of modern rail service in meeting the nation's transportation requirements. According to the legislation, the National Railroad Passenger Corporation, on or before May 1, 1971, was authorized to contract with any railroad to relieve it of the responsibility of providing intercity passenger service. Originally called *Railpax,* the new passenger service had to have a more descriptive name. It was decided to combine the words "American," "travel," and "track." The resultant combination was simple and easily remembered: *Amtrak.*

The period preceding May 1, 1971, was filled with negotiations with the railroads, selection of routes, incorporating the new organization, and a multitude of administrative activities. With one stroke, the railroads were relieved of an albatross around their necks, and Amtrak inherited the good as well as the bad. The *Metroliners* and the Northeast Corridor Project for high-speed ground transport was now an Amtrak show. Amtrak also took over the turbo trains that United Aircraft had produced. All of the plush trains in the west and Florida were now wearing the red, white, and blue of Amtrak, although a goodly share of them were dropped. The only exception to Amtrak's takeover of passenger service was the Southern Railroad, which elected to maintain its *Southern Crescent* and a few other runs. Commuter service was also retained by the railroads, because Amtrak's charter was only for intercity passenger service.

Amtrak also negotiated with the railroads for their existing passenger locomotives and equipment. Many of the streamlined, sleek General Motors E-8 locomotives from the Seaboard Coast Line, the Penn Central, the B&O/C&O, and the Illinois Central, all veterans of twenty years' service, were given over to Amtrak. For rolling stock, Amtrak took over the once proud but now dilapidated coaches and sleeper cars of the participating railroads—at least those that, it felt, could be refurbished. Most of these came from the Western railroads. With the mandate of Congress and the infusion of federal funds to help it, somehow, to create a miracle, Amtrak set out on its journey.

Upper left, three Amtrak SDP-40Fs sit side by side in the Washington, D.C., Ivy City locomotive terminal. Lower left, Amtrak #68, the southbound *Adirondack*, passes through Rensselaer, N.Y., in the snow and cold of the winter of 1977. Top right, the same *Adirondack*, this time operating in summer and in the mountain area of Cold Spring, N.Y. Bottom right, the morning *Metroliner* en route to New York through Lanham, Md. The Penn Central logo has already been removed from the lead unit, signifying the change in ownership. *(Dick Herbert photos)*

The Southern Railroad was the only intercity passenger carrier that did not negotiate a passenger service acquisition contract with Amtrak. Here, a single FP-7 sits northbound in the Alexandria station with a lone coach. Below, the classic E8s of the *Southern Crescent* sit next to two Seaboard Coast Line E8s at Washington's Ivy City locomotive terminal. On the opposite page, the new ownership of Amtrak shows up in this Seaboard Coast Line unit with a solitary patch marked "Amtrak." Eventually, this unit would be repainted and renumbered.

Amtrak

The early days of Amtrak's operation of the passenger service saw the growing pains of the infant railroad evident wherever passenger trains operated. Locomotives were still in the same color scheme of their former owners, except for a patch marked "Amtrak" placed wherever it could be conveniently seen. The coaches and sleepers were still attended by the same conductors and trainmen who had run them before the Amtrak takeover. After all, how could seniority be dislodged? And besides, who could run passenger trains better than experienced railroaders? Amtrak's long-range objective was to bring train travel up to a level of service at least comparable to that of the airlines. A central reservation system was installed, although this, too, had its growing pains when it first came in. Amtrak personnel soon became identified by a trademark of the red-white-and-blue arrow, along with the eye-catching uniforms. The slogans started: "Tracks are back;" "We're making trains worth travelling again." Amtrak hoped this would catch on.

At the left, these two photographs show the transition of the Amtrak image to equipment acquired from the railroads. At top, the northbound *Silver Star* rolls through Alexandria with two E-8s, one still in original Seaboard Coast Line markings, the trailing unit repainted in new Amtrak red and silver colors. At bottom, an already repainted unit heads the southbound *Silver Star* into the Alexandria station on its way to Florida.

The success of Amtrak depended heavily on whether it could convince the travelling public that the old, shabby image of passenger travel by train had been cleaned up by Amtrak's new type of service. To that end, Amtrak set up exhibitions wherever possible, such as Transpo '72 held at Dulles International Airport.

Soon, the new Amtrak identity began to emerge. To replace the aging E-8s acquired from the railroads, Amtrak ordered a fleet of over 100 SDP-40F locomotives from General Motors. These were 3000-horsepower adaptations of the SD-40, which had proven itself in millions of miles of freight service. The SDP-40F was streamlined and specially equipped for passenger service. The Amtrak color scheme now appeared everywhere across the nation. At top is an EMD builder's photograph of an SDP-40F. At bottom, the *Coast Starlight/Daylight* heads south along Puget Sound on its run to San Francisco.

The TurboTrain was looked upon as Amtrak's big winner in the Northeast Corridor. With *Metroliner* providing high-speed passenger service in the Washington-to-New York market, the TurboTrain was to be its high-speed counterpart in the Boston-to-New York segment. Here, the TurboTrain is on exhibition at Transpo '72 in Washington D.C.

The *Panama Limited*, once the Illinois Central's crack overnight sleeper from Chicago to New Orleans, now has a new owner and new equipment. Behind two new SDP-40Fs, the *Panama Limited* backs out of Union Station in Chicago on its departure ritual. It will then move forward over the overpass shown in the background and eventually find its way south to New Orleans along the route of the Illinois Central Gulf. Of the many railroad stations serving passenger traffic in Chicago, only Union Station is used by Amtrak. All of the rest have been abandoned or are used for commuter traffic. *(Photo by Howard Ameling)*

The National Limited used to be a famous B&O trademark—but now, Amtrak operates it over the route of the Penn Central. Here an SDP-40F and an E8 team up to race the *National Limited* westbound past Port Tower at Newport, Pa. *(Photo by John Taibi)*

The camera of John Taibi caught the eastbound *National Limited* rolling past the stone station at Mifflin, Pa., behind another SDP-40F and an ex-Penn Central E8, with a Fourth of July holiday extra consist.

Amtrak's high-speed service soon became one of its trademarks. The visions of the Pennsylvania Railroad and its high-speed Northeast Corridor project saw the expansion of *Metroliner* service to as many as fourteen trains a day each way—but now this was an Amtrak operation. The TurboTrains also found a new route to Parkersburg, W. Va., but only for a brief moment, as the traffic volume was too low to maintain the service. At top, the Parkersburg *Turbo* races through Rockville, Md., on its westward run. Below, the southbound *Metroliner* begins to slow down on its approach towards the Capital Beltway station at Lanham, Md. At right, some *Metroliners* never stop at the Capital Beltway station, as shown by this one blasting southward at 60 mph.

From the Midwest prairies to New England and the Hudson River country rolled the bulk of Amtrak service. Above, three F-3 units still in the original color schemes of the Great Northern and the Northern Pacific (now merged into the Burlington Northern) haul the westbound *Empire Builder* out of the Union Station complex in Chicago in September 1972. Below, local Amtrak #405 is pictured at Springfield, Mass., by Tom Hildreth.

Tom Hildreth also caught the eastbound *Lake Shore Limited* passing Five Mile Pond at Springfield, Mass., on a rainy day in March 1977. Below, the eastbound *Washington Irving* rolls towards Harmon, N.Y., from a view atop the tunnels at Oscawanna, N.Y., on the once-famed Water Level Route of the New York Central. According to John Taibi, who photographed this scene, this stretch of track, which once carried such famous trains as the *Commodore Vanderbilt*, the *Twentieth Century Limited*, and the *Empire State Express*, now has a new list of unfamiliar names, such as the *Salt City Express*, the *Niagara Rainbow*, and others. Amtrak evidently saw fit to retain only one name—the *Lake Shore Limited*—to remind rail buffs of the glory that once was the New York Central.

588
Amtrak

310 W. POLK BUILDING

The growing Amtrak soon began to have some serious operating problems. The SDP-40F soon became identified as the cause of many derailments of Amtrak trains. On the Penn Central, the *Broadway Limited* derailed three times in a three-month period. Similar derailments occurred on the routes of the Santa Fe, the Seaboard Coast Line, and other rail lines. The cause was soon identified: it was the excessive sidesway by the six-axle trucks at the trailing end of these locomotives. Critics asserted that these SDP-40Fs were only freight locomotives reconfigured to serve as passenger locomotives—and that was a different type of service. At any rate, with a commitment for over 100 of these locomotives, Amtrak sent many of them to the Illinois Central Gulf's Paducah locomotive shops, and eventually many more would be returned to EMD's La Grange, Ill., plant as trade-ins for a newer type of passenger locomotive. Some railroads, such as Conrail, had outlawed the SDP-40F completely, while others made it operate within severe speed limits. Small wonder that Amtrak had to re-order.

At top left, the eastbound *Broadway Limited* was running 1½ hours late when John Taibi photographed it entering the Harrisburg, Pa., station. At Harrisburg, the SDP-40Fs will be cut off for electric-powered GG-1s and the train split up—part going to Washington, D.C., and the other section headed for New York City. At bottom left, the *Southwest Limited* heads for Los Angeles out of Chicago. Below, the northbound St. Petersburg-to-New York *Champion* races by the Charleston, S.C., station. *(Photos also by Howard Ameling)*

The operating restrictions imposed on the SDP-40F left many Amtrak trains in a power bind. Once again Amtrak had to depend on the aging E8 to haul its standard-weight trains on many parts of the nation's rail network. In some cases, these locomotives would fail, causing delays of up to twelve hours on some trains. In many cases, freight locomotives of the carrying railroad would be pressed into service to get Amtrak through. Still, Amtrak kept on rolling, and it soon became evident that the passenger train was far from finished—particularly when the oil fields of the Middle East stopped fueling the American automobile in 1973. All of a sudden, people found that gas pumps running dry was a far worse problem than Amtrak running late.

Conrail had outlawed completely the SDP-40F from its rails, and all of Amtrak's East-West service had to depend on the E-8. At top, SD-45 #6220, a freight locomotive, helps out the eastbound *National Limited*, running three hours late, through Duncannon, Pa. *(Photo by John Gabriel)* Below, the eastbound *National Limited* clears the tower at Duncannon, Pa., running twenty minutes early, a rare occasion indeed. *(Photo by John Taibi)*

VIEW
440

Howard Ameling has photographed two different *Lake Shore Limited* scenes through Toledo, Ohio. Above, running late, the *Lake Shore* needs assistance from Conrail #3111. Below, one of the few SDP-40F units still working on Conrail trails an E8 on a westbound *Lake Shore Limited*. At one time, the New York Central used to operate the original *Lake Shore Limited* on a sixteen-hour schedule out of New York City. The present Amtrak schedule is twenty hours, due to bad track.

A completely new idea in travel by passenger train was unfolded not by Amtrak but by a new corporation known as Auto-Train. One of the experiments carried out by the Department of Commerce in 1968 indicated that an auto-ferry-type passenger service in the United States would be feasible, and that the venture should be pursued by private industry. However, with the oncoming divestiture of passenger service from the railroads, railroad management was the last in line to back such a venture. In 1969, Eugene Kerik Garfield left government service to form the Auto-Train Corporation with a group of private investors. It was the first new privately owned railroad corporation in over fifty years. Because neither the railroads nor Amtrak would develop the concept, it remained for Auto-Train to jump in, feet first.

And it did just that. Fifteen-year operating agreements were signed with the Seaboard Coast Line and the Richmond, Fredericksburg, and Potomac railroads that provided for the operation of Auto-Train over the rights-of-way of the two railroads. Since the Santa Fe and the Western Pacific were getting out of the passenger business in the west, they had available some of the finest vista-domed coaches in the country. These were purchased, as were a number of sleeping cars from the Santa Fe and the Union Pacific. Because the Canadian railroads were already operating auto transporters on some of their trains, automobile carriers were obtained from the Canadian National Railway. An order was placed with General Electric for five 3600-horsepower U-36B locomotives. Swindell-Dressler, Inc., drew up plans for terminals at Lorton, Va., and Sanford, Fla.

Perhaps the greatest show of confidence in the new venture came from the public itself. On July 15, 1971, a public offering was made of its stock. Within the first day, the offering was completely sold out. At $10 a share, Auto-Train had raised $6.3 million in capital. In the ensuing four-and-a-half months, Garfield and his associates literally put the carrier on its wheels. The auto carriers and the passenger equipment were completely refurbished by Pullman-Standard in Chicago. The new terminals were built at Lorton and Sanford. An employee staff of train service directors, passenger assistants, and train hostesses was recruited and trained. Finally, on December 6, 1971, a new dimension in rail passenger service was introduced when the first Auto-Train, carrying passengers and their automobiles, departed the Lorton Terminal for the fifteen-and-a-half-hour run to Sanford.

The northbound Auto-Train has already left the RF&P main line and glides into the Lorton, Va., terminal, with the auto carriers immediately behind the twin GE U-36B diesels. Top right, the auto carriers are already opened, and the unloading crews supervise the drive-off of all of the cars to the pick-up point where their owners will depart, northbound on I-95. Bottom right, the passengers are reunited with their automobiles.

At top left, cars arrive at the Lorton Terminal for the afternoon Auto-Train to Sanford. They are inspected and checked in for the trip, while, at a service desk, the passengers are checked in and receive car assignments. Cars then proceed up the ramp to the auto carriers.

Following pages: a hostess welcomes arriving passengers aboard. U-36B #4006 sits for a portrait; several views of the vista-domed cars and the service that awaits the Florida-bound traveller.

auto-train
at-11

4006
4006
4006

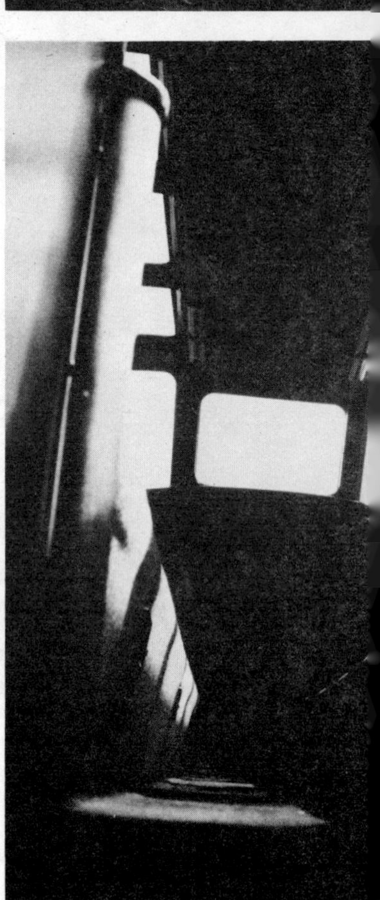

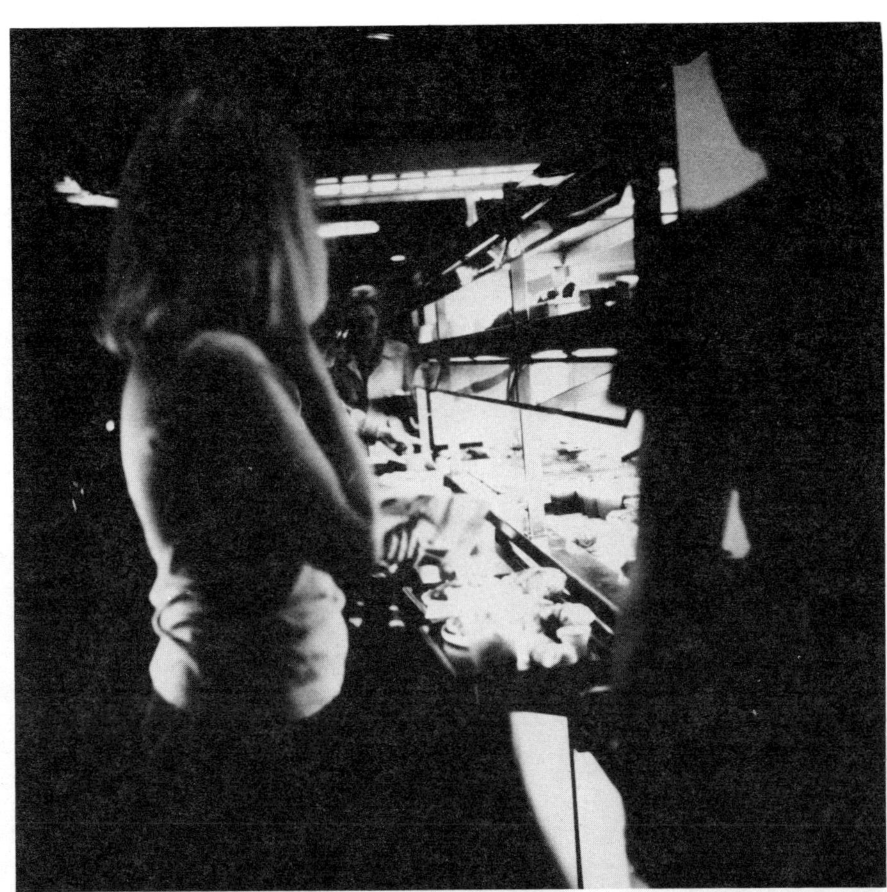

The locomotive has already coupled onto the auto carriers and is now proceeding forward on the yard track, where it will couple onto the vista-domed cars at the right of the photo.

Below is a combination carrier and caboose, caught by Howard Ameling's camera in Sanford, Fla. Auto-Train soon expanded into the Midwest market, establishing a service from Louisville, Ky., to Sanford, Fla. With service more personalized than that of the airlines, and with more innovations than the railroads were ever able to conceive in their lifetime, Auto-Train caused a shock wave through the transportation industry. However, economics and operating headaches soon overtook the young, aggressive carrier. Several costly derailments left a bad impact, as well as a lack of patronage on the Louisville service. Auto-Train cancelled four additional locomotives it had ordered from General Electric and thus they became the first new motive power to go over to Conrail. The cheap, bargain prices for auto rental in Florida made travel by Auto-Train costly by comparison, resulting in losses of revenue. Perhaps the biggest factor was the completion of I-95 through most of the way between the north and the south. Auto-Train was hard pressed to find the formula to get people out of their automobiles and onto the Lorton-to-Sanford run.

A dramatic view of the *Water Level Express* at Bear Mountain.

Meanwhile, back at Amtrak, the next wave of modernization had begun. The United Aircraft TurboTrain had initially demonstrated the utility of this type of passenger mover, but over a longer period of time had not performed well. Eventually, it was phased out. In the meantime, Amtrak became impressed with the ANF-Frangeco turbotrains ordered by the French National Railways, and in 1973 ordered two trains for initial service. This was followed by an additional eight trains that were ordered by 1975. These trains were capable of sustained speeds of up to 125 miles per hour on conventional track, and they were operated consistantly at that speed in France. Above left, one of the trains pauses in Pittsburgh en route to its Chicago base of operation. The Turboliners were placed in Chicago-Detroit and Chicago-Milwaukee service. At lower left, a Chicago-Milwaukee run enters Union Station in Chicago. Above, #362 leaves Chicago for Detroit. ***(Both photos by Howard Ameling.)***

The success of the French Turboliners encouraged Amtrak to order additional Turboliners from Rohr Corporation, which now was producing the trains based upon the French design. As a result, Amtrak expanded its Turboliner service to upstate New York, operating between New York City, Albany, and Buffalo. Above, #62, the *Salt City Express*, glides toward New York beside the frozen-solid Hudson River in the winter of 1977, at Peekskill, New York. *(photo by John Taibi)*

Occasionally, rarities show up along the tracks if one waits long enough. In this photo, Howard Ameling captured the westbound *Lake Shore Limited* hauling a powerless #153 Turboliner unit through Toledo in the dead of winter. It is evidently en route to Amtrak's Brighton Park, Ill., service facility.

Encouraged by the operating performance of *Metroliner*, Amtrak made its biggest move in 1975 with the introduction of the Amfleet service—a complete departure from conventional passenger equipment designed to bring the maximum in comfort for day train travel. The order was for 492 Amfleet cars, consisting of Amcoach, Amclub, Amcafe, and Amdinette units. The coaches featured spacious seating, drop-down tables for eating or working, ample luggage accommodations, and superior air conditioning systems. Amfleet was introduced to the Northeast Corridor to complement the *Metroliner* service, but soon was inaugurated all over the country. Above left, the newly refurbished *Metroliner* races through the Capital Beltway station at Lanham, Md. Lower left, the *Shenandoah* heads northbound at Silver Spring, Md., behind a General Electric P30CH designed specifically to pull Amfleet equipment on non-electrified routes. Above, the *Blue Ridge* rolls westbound at Harper's Ferry, W. Va.—A new train in an old setting.

The success of the Amfleet equipment and the Turboliners soon made it apparent that this equipment could be put in service not only in the Northeast but everywhere on Amtrak's routes. Amfleet-equipped trains were introduced in the South on trains such as the *Palmetto,* which ran to the Carolinas, or the *Colonial,* which ran to Newport News, Va. In the Midwest, Amfleet appeared on the *Inter-American,* the *Cardinal,* the *Ann Rutledge,* and many other trains, which ran to St. Louis, Duluth, Laredo, Tex., Catlettsburg, Ky., and Minneapolis. In the far West, there were the Amfleet-equipped *Pacific International* and the *San Diegans,* which operated in the Los Angeles-San Diego Corridor.

For the shorter-distance runs such as the New York-Boston service, Amtrak operated high-density Amfleet equipment. Coaches seated eighty-four persons, and food service was offered stand-up style in Amcafe coaches. For the longer-distance trains such as the Washington-to-Cincinnati *Shenandoah,* Amfleet equipment consisted of sixty-seat Amcoaches, which afforded full stretch-out leg room, and Amdinette service, where patrons could obtain hot meals in a modernized dining-car setting.

The changeover to Amfleet service was accompanied by a revamping of Amtrak's locomotive fleet. In the electrified district of the Northeast, Amtrak placed in service a fleet of 25 E-60P six-axle locomotives built by General Electric Corporation. GE also delivered to Amtrak twenty-five diesel-electric locomotives designated as the P30CH, each unit capable of 3000 horsepower and specifically designed for non-electrified routes. These P30CH locomotives were originally used to serve non-electrified territority out of the Ivy City terminal at Washington, D.C., but were subsequently dispatched to other parts of Amtrak's network. At one time, they were loaned to the Soutern Pacific for its San Francisco Bay Area commuter operations. A small fleet of General Motors F40PHR locomotives assigned to Amfleet service between New York and Boston was augmented by an eventual 120 additional units delivered to the road as trade-ins for the discredited SDP-40F, which had been slowed down to 40 miles per hour by order of the railroads that had experienced the derailment problem. Thus, Amtrak was gradually renovating not only its fleet of cars but the locomotives that pulled them.

These Amtrak-furnished photographs show the interiors of the new equipment. Above is an illustration of the parlor car section of the French-built Turboliners, showing a two-and-one seating arrangement across a wide aisle. Below, a view of an Amdinette unit showing the food serving area and the dining table spaces.

In the electrified line stretching from Washington to New York, Amtrak not only took over the operation of the trains but also the responsibility for the line as well. To pull the new Amfleet trains as well as the remainder of the conventionally equipped trains, Amtrak introduced a fleet of new 5000-horsepower General Electric locomotives. Above, the conductor and engineer of the northbound *Colonial* check signals at Lanham, Md. At left, a glistening new stainless-steel Amclub car sits behind #958 at Capital Beltway Station. Opposite page, Amtrak #141, the southbound *Bankers*, arrives at Capital Beltway station. Below, the northbound *Merchants Limited* rips by the Ivy City locomotive terminal in northeast Washington, D.C.

The camera of Dick Herbert has captured some spectacular scenes of the new Amtrak in operation. At top left, one of the last photos of the United Aircraft *TurboTrains* in operation, this one at New Milford, Conn. Bottom left, the eastbound Turboliner-equipped *Salt Lake City Express* winds its way over the ice-filled Hudson from a view high atop the Bear Mountain Bridge. Above, Amtrak's new French Turbotrain. Below, the eastbound *Blue Ridge* is shown passing over the bridge at Harper's Ferry, W. Va.

As the year 1980 began, the passenger train was again in a dramtic state of delicate balance. The tremors of the energy crises of 1973 and 1979 had eased, although the energy problem hadn't really gone away. With pretroleum once again reaching our shores from the Middle East, the passenger train's role as an emergency resource began to recede. For all of its innovation, Auto-Train was virtually on the ropes. Faced by the airline fare wars on one hand and the inexpensive car rental rates offering unlimited mileage in Florida, the lucrative market Auto-Train once enjoyed was not one it had to hold onto. At its most recent stockholders' meeting, it was stated that another derailment would hold disastrous consequences. Serious questions were raised about Auto-Train's fare structures, and about its choice of origin and destination terminals, the Midwest service had long passed, and now the East Coast-to-Florida service was digging in for survival.

Amtrak was also having its problems, but, instead of anxious stockholders, the Department of Transportation and Congress were the ones raising eyebrows about the nationwide passenger service. While the Northeast Corridor was receiving the full benefit of a massive Federal program designed to improve passenger train service in the highest-population-density areas, the rest of the Amtrak network was being considered for a significant downgrading, with many trains being discontinued. On the eve of the gasoline shortage of 1979, Secretary of Transportation Brock Adams was at the forefront of the Carter Administration's drive to cut 43% of Amtrak's route-miles. When the energy crisis hit with its full fury, Amtrak's telephones literally rang off the wall. Compared to May 1978, when Amtrak received one million calls, in May 1979 it received 6.8 million calls. The *Southwestern Limited* and the *Coast Starlight* were sold out weeks in advance. The Carter Administration found itself in the paradoxical position of wanting to ration gasoline on one hand, while also wanting to cut back the energy-efficient service Amtrak could provide on the other hand.

A public opinion survey conducted for Amtrak disclosed that many people—in particular, those living along five designated train corridors—rated Amtrak very highly. Although a majority still felt that passenger train service was not what it used to be, and only 9 percent of the likely travellers living in Amtrak-served corridors felt the train would be a first choice, a very large percentage of potential travellers indicated that they would become train users if the service continued to improve. Thus, while cars and planes continued to dominate in the five rail-served corridors—San Diego to Los Angeles, New York to Buffalo, Portland to Seattle, Washington to Boston, and Chicago to Detroit—the train had the potential for drawing ridership. Unfortunately, this survey indicated that this drawing power might be from the intercity bus companies . . . and these bus operators were beginning to complain vociferously that Federal subsidizing of Amtrak was unfair competition to the bus. The goal of getting people out of energy-extravagant transportation modes such as the car and the jet airplane was not working out.

In the meantime, Amtrak continued to make improvements to its equipment, and, in addition, its full attention now centered on the Northeast Corridor Improvement Project (abbreviated to NECIP by governmentese nomenclature). This project was the most advanced attempt to restore high-speed passenger service to the rails. While negotiations were in progress with General Motors' Electro-Motive Division for a Swedish model 7000-horsepower electric locomotive to be known as the AEM-7, the 1930-vintage GG-1s of the Pennsylvania Railroad continued to pull Amtrak through the New York-to-Washington route. The remnants of the SDP-40Fs still pulled the Florida-bound standardweight coaches and sleepers, while new F40 diesel-electric locomotives were being ordered. Amtrak's modification program still rolls on.

A pair of GG-1s—the lead unit painted in Amtrak silver, red, and blue—waits to depart from Trenton, N.J., with the westbound *National Limited*.

Railroading in the Northeast is not without hazards, as this Amtrak F40PHR demonstrates. Because of vandals throwing rocks from trackside and from overpasses, Amtrak has installed wire grilles over the cab windows of all locomotives operating in the Northeast. To the locomotive engineer behind the controls, it might seem that he has been placed behind bars—but eyesight lost through flying glass can never be regained.

At left, the southbound *Silver Star* eases out of Alexandria, Va., behind two SDP-40Fs operating on the Richmond, Fredericksburg, and Potomac line out of Washington, D.C.

276
Amtrak
Amtrak

The F40PHR became the most extensively used locomotive throughout the Amtrak system. On the West Coast, through the Midwest, and in the Southeast, these locomotives became the major source of power assigned to pull the new Amfleet equipment. The *Colonial* is shown on the opposite page with its three-car consist from Newport News, Va. At bottom, the people assembled at trackside in Rockville, Maryland are not waiting for the *Blue Ridge*, shown here. They are awaiting the arrival of the steam-powered *Chessie Special*, following behind.

The new and the humorous side of Amtrak: a side view and a front view of Amtrak's experimental Swedish-built Rc4a locomotive. This is the prototype unit for a fleet of 30 locomotives to be delivered in 1980-1981, with an additional 17 locomotives to follow later. Known as the AEM-7, these locomotives will replace all of the GG-1's and possibly the E60's in the Washington-to-Boston Northeast Corridor. The AEM-7 will be built by Electro-Motive with major components from ASEA, a Swedish manufacturer of electrical components.

Meanwhile, an ex-Pennsy caternary repair car painted "AMTK" on its sides and a smiling face up front heads through Trenton, N.J.

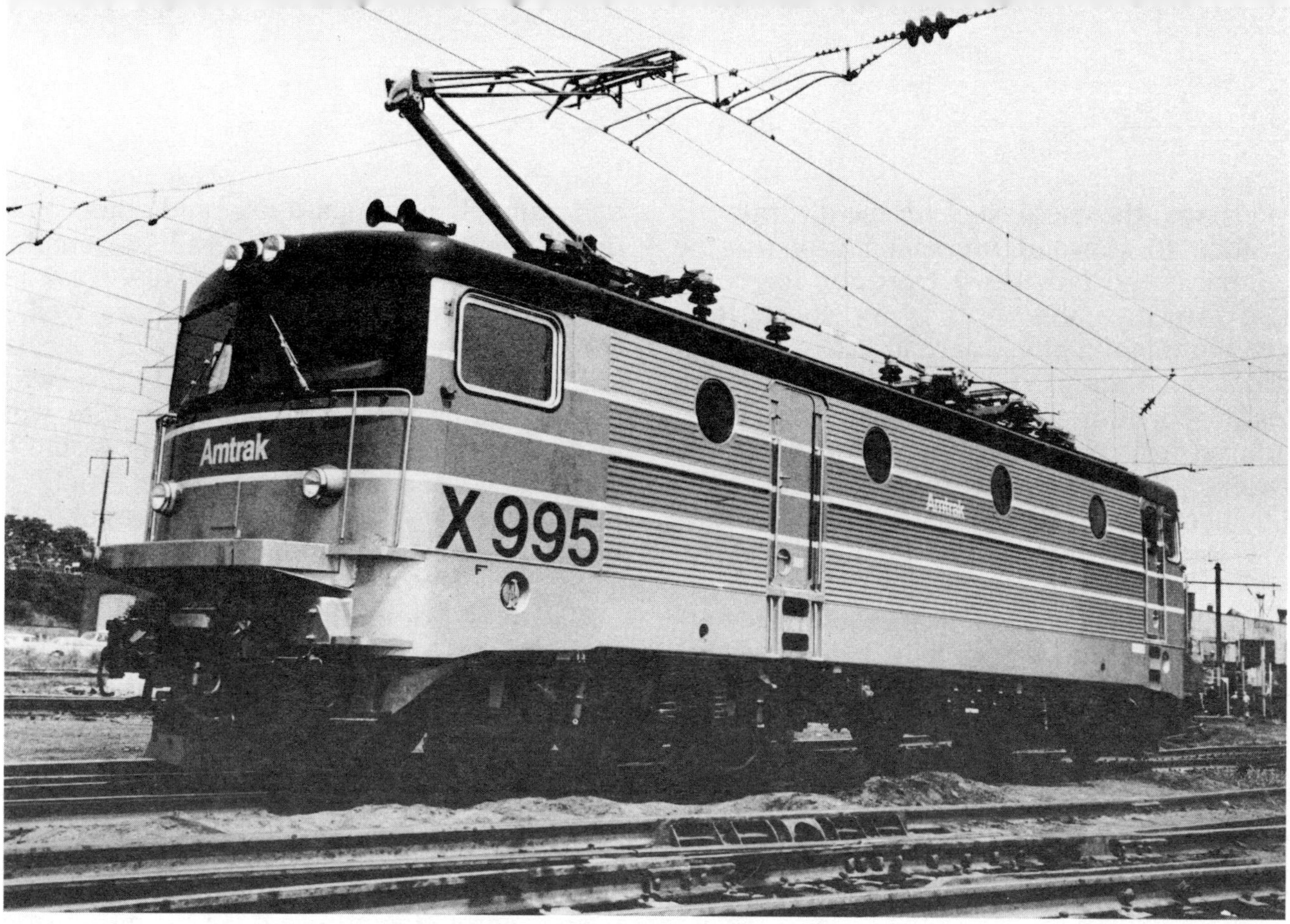
Amtrak
X 995
Amtrak

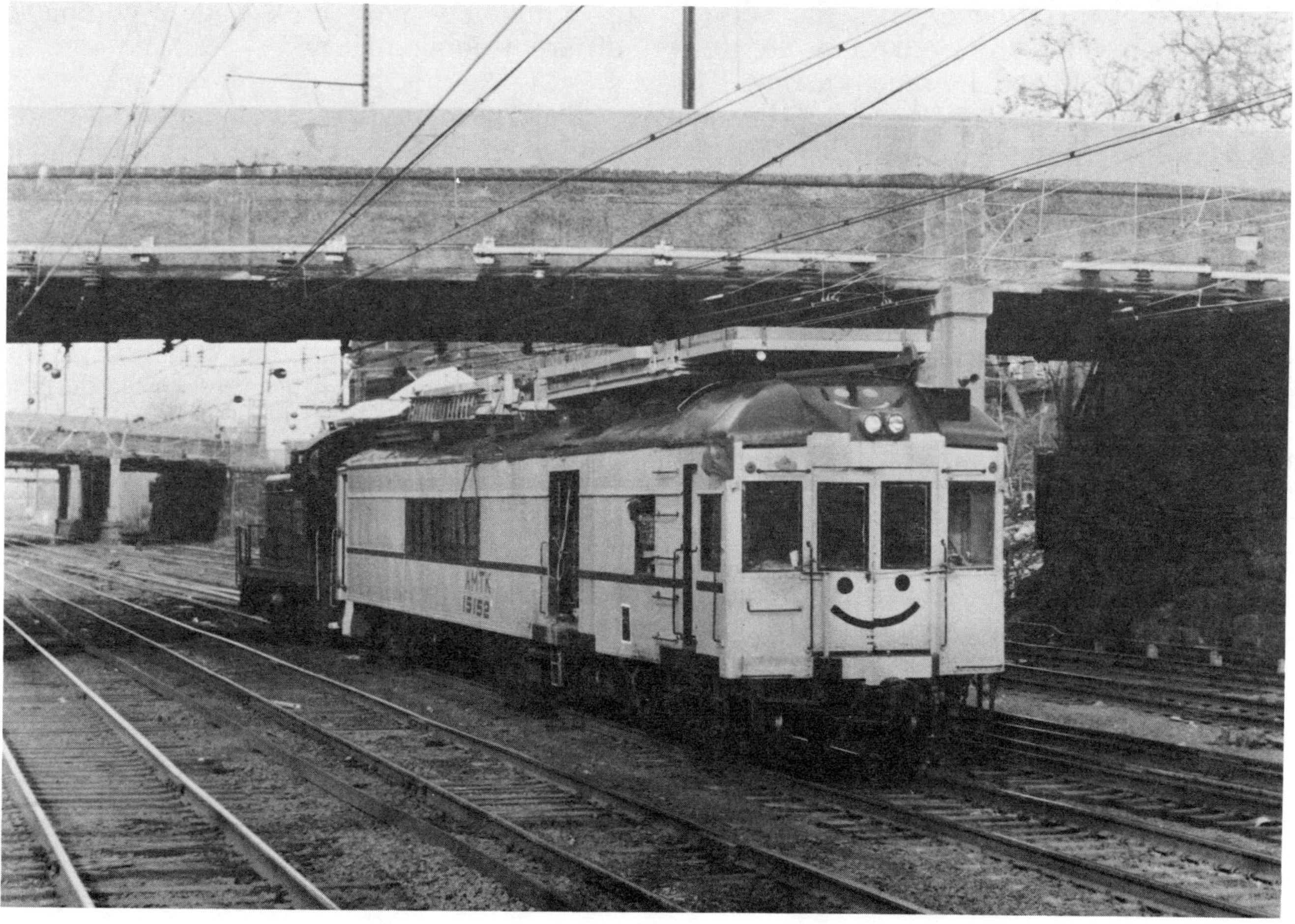
AMTK
15152

Perhaps the boldest and most dramatic advance in railroad implementation in the country is the Northeast Corridor Improvement Project, called NECIP for short. Recognizing that the physical roadbed, signalling, and environment of the Washington-to-Boston corridor was 100 years old and had suffered from the deterioration of its former owners, the Pennsylvania and the New Haven railroads, Congress passed the Railroad Revitalization and Regulatory Reform Act of 1976, more commonly known as the 4R Act. This Act had among its goals the establishment of regular passenger service between Boston and New York scheduled for 3 hours and 40 minutes and from New York to Washington in 2 hours and 40 minutes. The Act authorized $1.6 billion for improvements to the roadbed and $150 million for fencing and other improvements, the latter funds to be matched by state and local sources.

Under the NECIP mandate, the service would be provided from 6:00 A.M. to 10:00 P.M. according to the 4R requirements. The system would be designed to carry 21.8 million passengers annually. This figure forecast the diverting of 1.35 million trips from air and 2.5 million trips from automobiles.

The NECIP operations were undertaken at full speed during the beginning of 1978. Along the entire route from Washington to Boston, bright orange ballast cars, tie-carrying gondola cars, and continuous welded-rail cars appeared. Amtrak acquired a fleet of bright orange locomotives to haul all these cars. Scores of track construction workers appeared almost at every mile with a vast array of equipment, bringing construction and repair to miles of trackage that had only known the neglectful policy of its previous owners. Contained in this revitalization program were a whole series of track improvements, bridge and tunnel modifications, and the laying down of continuous welded rail. A complete program of electrification from New Haven to Boston was to be accomplished, as well as the upgrading of the remainder of the electrical power plant the rest of the way. Modifications to the signalling system were also planned. Every grade crossing would be eliminated, and the entire route would be fenced and protected against straying animals, transients, and the inevitable vandals.

The most astounding piece of equipment on the entire project is the Track Laying System. The Track Laying System is a series of machines that are used to totally renew a railroad roadbed from the ballast to the rail alignment. Track Laying System can renew roadbed three-and-a-half times as fast as conventional methods. Instead of the conventional wooden ties, the Track Laying System uses concrete ties, thus giving the old railroad a completely new look and a completely different riding quality.

The Track Laying System has as its central component a $1.5 million P-811 track laying machine, which stretches a full quarter of a mile. One end of it rides on the old rails and old roadbed, while the other end rolls on continuous welded rail set upon the new concrete ties. It replaces old rails and crossties with new rails and concrete ties at a rate of ten ties per minute covering a distance of 1200 feet per hour. The entire process consists of undercutting the old roadbed and cleaning the ballast, exchanging the old rail with continuous welded rail, and then exchanging the old wooden ties with the concrete replacement ties. There are flatcars in the system which hold the old ties that have been removed and the new ties to be installed. A gantry crane rides on top of these supply cars, exchanging the new for the old.

Behind the P-811, rail clips and insulators are put into place, new ballast is added, and surfacing machinery aligns the track. A total of 400 miles of track are scheduled for upgrading with the TLS.

When the dust has settled and the construction equipment has been rolled off the tracks, the NECIP will have brought to the rails an entirely new concept in passenger travel. What started with the New Tokkaido Line in Japan as the demonstration that it could be done, what *Metroliner* tried to do with only partial success, now will finally come to pass. A fleet of 46 lightweight AEM-7 7000-hp locomotives, pulling trains of up to eight modified Amfleet-type cars at speeds of 120 miles per hour, will race up and down the Northeast Corridor. Whether this will attract the traveller from automobiles and jet aircraft remains to be seen.

These Amtrak photographs show the Track Laying System in full operation. Above is an overall view of the TLS, showing the supply cars and the main unit. Opposite, the gantry crane is stacking the old ties removed from the roadbed.

AMTK 15590

At the rate of ten ties per minute, the old wooden ties are pulled up from the roadbed and the new ties are put down. Note that the rail is spread out to allow tie replacement to take place. The rails are then realigned over the new ties and, finally, the new roadbed is secured. Note the difference between the new track versus the old.

A two-car Amfleet-equipped *Hilltopper* pauses briefly in the old Alexandria, Virginia station en route to its final destination, Washington D.C.

This is where NECIP is headed: a fleet of 120 mile-per-hour trains operating between Washington and Boston, linking the two cities in six-and-a-half hours' travel time or less. Amtrak's new high-speed, lightweight electric locomotives will combine high horsepower with light weight to pull trains of up to eight cars. The first two locomotives have already been delivered and are being tested at Pueblo, Colorado, and on the electrified Washington-to New York portion of Amtrak's Northeast Corridor.

4
Conrail

By the beginning of 1973, it became clear to everybody and his dog that not only was the Penn Central system in a state of coma, but the entire railroad network in the Northeast was ready to collapse. Hurricane Agnes had given the *coup de grace* to the Penn Central, which simply could not raise enough money to make repairs to its battered system, and ultimately was facing problems even meeting its payroll. During 1972, the number of railroads in bankruptcy became alarming. No less than six railroads—the Penn Central, the Central Railroad of New Jersey, the Lehigh Valley, the Reading, the Erie-Lackawanna, and the Lehigh and Hudson River Railroad—had filed for bankruptcy. The Nixon Administration wrestled with the problem of whether to find some sort of a reorganization, nationalize the entire rail region, or else let liquidation dissolve the Penn Central and force a complete shutdown of operations.

Thus, the problems facing the railroads of the Northeast—problems that had their roots deep in the technological revolution that developed after World War II—finally came to a head. The Penn Central merger, attempting to stave off these problems, caused an even worse problem because of the incompatibility of the two railroads and their operating personnel. The problem thus became a national issue. Congress passed the Regional Rail Reorganization Act of 1973 after long and sometimes bitter hearings. The United States Railway Association (USRA) was created under this act, with the mandate to reorganize the bankrupt rail lines of the Northeast and Midwest into a viable rail transportation system. One of the provisions of the act was the creation of some form of Consolidated Railroad Corporation as a private corporation, receiving a federal investment of some $2.1 billion to restore the operating capability of those lines essential for continued transport in the critically affected areas. Thus, Conrail was conceived.

It took the formation of two systems plans—a Preliminary System Plan, issued February 26, 1975, and a Final System Plan, issued July 28, 1975, and accepted by Congress on November 9, 1975—to formulate an analysis of the problem and present a recommended route structure and plan of acquisition of the bankrupt properties by Conrail. The plans called for establishment of three principal railroad systems in the Northeast and Midwest. One was Conrail, which had been formed by the consolidation of all of the essential portions of the bankrupt systems; the others were Chessie and the Norfolk and Western, the two profitable, self-sustaining routes. Conrail, according to the Final System Plan, must also be self-sustaining, meet adequate regional rail transportation needs, improve the Northeast Corridor's high-speed passenger transportation capability, and achieve efficiency in train operations, to cite a few of the objectives.

As the Penn Central accelerated towards its final doomsday run, the reorganization processes also accelerated. On January 28, 1976, Congress passed the Railroad Revitalization and Regulatory Reform Act, which amended the original Rail Act and officially gave the go-ahead for the formation of Conrail. On March 12, 1976, Conrail concluded the financing arrangement with USRA, giving it access to $2.1 billion in government investment funds. With Edward G. Jordan, the president of USRA, as Chairman and Chief Executive Officer and Richard D. Spence as President and Chief Operating Officer, Activation Day was April 1, 1976. On that date, all rail operations of the Penn Central, the Erie-Lackawanna, the Lehigh Valley, the Reading, the Central of New Jersey, and the tiny Lehigh and Hudson River Railroad became one system—Conrail.

The camera of Dick Herbert captured this dramatic night photograph of 6;4022, an ex-Erie-Lackawanna passenger unit, painted in the new Conrail colors. While Conrail has no intercity passenger service, it sill has its passenger-type locomotives for special assignments. Opposite, the caboose of a westbound freight leaving Enola that is temporarily halted sees a slow-moving train of empty PEPCO coal cars inch up forward in the early-morning haze. At opposite bottom, three locomotives roar westward at Enola—the first from the Penn Central, the second an ex-CNJ unit that has already been repainted and renumbered.

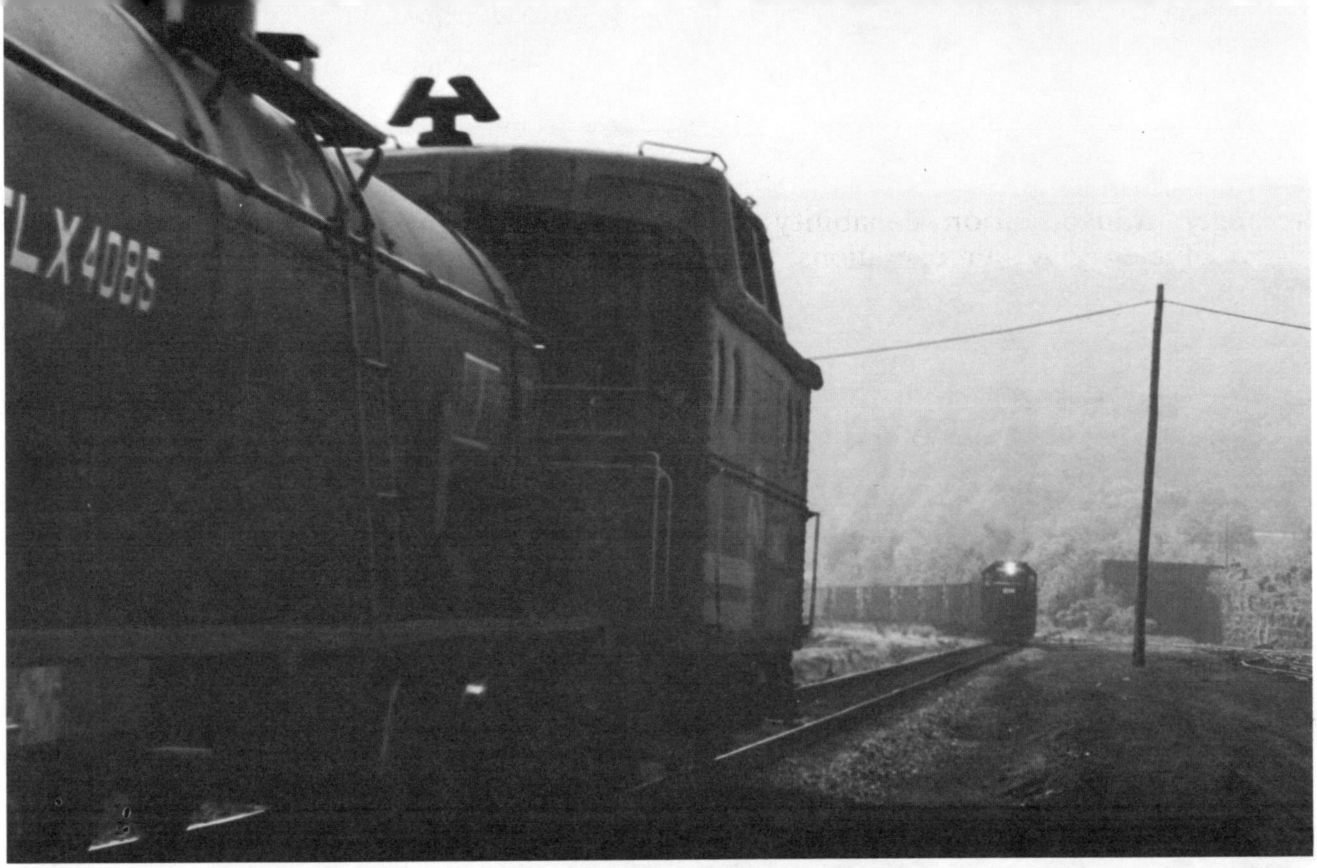
LX 4085

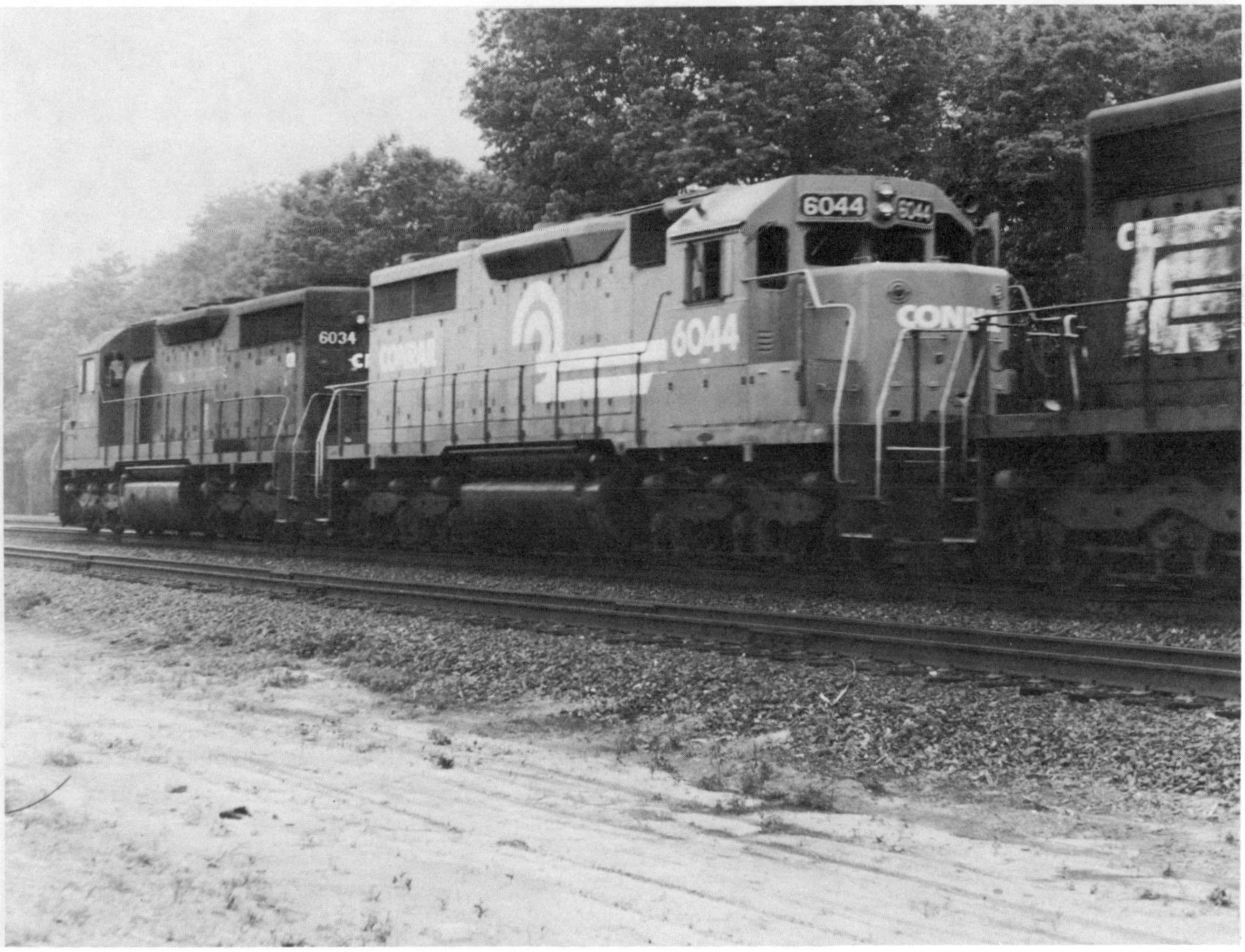
6044
6034
CONRAIL
6044

For the rail enthusiast, Conrail's formation created some of the wildest power combinations imaginable—the units of six railroads appeared, some re-lettered "CR," others repainted Conrail blue, and still others brand-new. Above, a westbound TV-9 rips by west of Harrisburg, Pa., with two new GP-40-2s, while an ex-Erie-Lackawanna GP-35 heads east with a load of coal bound for Pennsylvania Power and Light Co. Opposite, a Reading six-axle unit heads east with two PC units at Niles, Ohio. *(Photo by Howard Ameling)*

5300
5300

6114

At left, a local freight servicing the Port Jervis and Binghamton area heads east behind two E-L F7s. *(Photo by John Taibi)* At top, Howard Ameling photographed this leased Canadian National unit at Cleveland, Ohio. Bottom, John Taibi captured these three LV GP-38s at night at Sayre, Pa.

After Activation Day, the business of restoring the new rail system began. Motive power was one of the most critical issues. The bankrupt railroads had postponed all maintenance of these movers of freight, and, as a result, the serviceable locomotives of each of the bankrupt roads soon found themselves scattered all over the system. Conrail trains took on weird mixtures of road names. In addition, other railroads not in the consolidation also showed up. Because Conrail was so short of locomotives, it leased many units from the Canadian National, the Chicago and North Western, the Southern Pacific, and a host of other roads. Result: Almost anything could show up at any time—and it usually did.

The shops at Altoona, Hollidaysburg, Collinwood, Meadville, DeWitt, and a host of other names familiar to railroaders began to work night and day to refurbish the locomotives and rolling stock of the stricken railroads. In 1976, some 780 diesel locomotives were rehabilitated. The plans for 1977 called for an additional 900+ units to be rebuilt. In addition to using its own shops, Conrail sent a number of units for complete rebuilding at the Paducah, Ky., shops of the Illinois Central Gulf.

In addition to rebuilding its existing locomotive fleet, Conrail also went shopping for new motive power. According to roster statistics published by *Extra 2200 South*, a magazine dealing with the reporting of railway locomotive characteristics, Conrail had ordered a total of 392 new units as of June 1980. 167 of them were the six-axle SD40-2 units built by Electro-Motive Division, 106 were the four-axle, 3000-hp GP40-2, and 219 were the lesser-horsepower GP38-2 and GP-15. General Electric furnished another 151 units, mostly the B23-7 type. By early 1980, the locomotive situation at Conrail had improved to the point where it could lease units to power-short railroads such as the Soo Line, the Chicago and Northwestern, and the Santa Fe.

Car rebuilding also was done on a round-the-clock basis, with the most critical need being for hopper cars to meet the rising need for coal energy sources. Nearly 12,000 cars were refurbished in 1976. New rolling stock was also ordered in thousand-lot quantities from 1976 to 1980, with the preponderance of them being hopper cars for increasing coal traffic, and covered hopper cars for commodities such as grain and chemicals. The piggyback fleet of trailer-vans and the specially equipped flat cars to haul them was also increased.

The track rehabilitation program also showed good progress. Almost 8,000 miles of track had been subject to reduced speeds due to deterioration of the roadbed. At the end of 1976, approximately ten percent of these routes had been rehabilitated. By mid-1980, nearly a third of the system had been upgraded. As an example of this improvement, Amtrak was now able to operate Amfleet equipment at speeds approaching 100 mph, and Turbo equipment at speeds in excess of 100 mph on the Conrail line between Albany and Amsterdam, New York. For freight shippers, this meant an immediate improvement in delivery times that could only result in averting the growing movement off the rails and into trucks. Shippers were slowly coming back, and the overall climate was picking up. Indeed, the presence of the $2.1 billion—now augmented to an authorized $3.3 billion—in government investment funds was being felt.

At the Conrail locomotive facility in Altoona, GE U-25B locomotives from the Penn Central sit side by side in various stages of rebuilding. ***(Photo courtesy of Conrail)*** **Below, a set of rails is being unloaded and stacked west of Harrisburg for formation into welded rail to be used in refurbishing of track on the line between Altoona and Harrisburg.**

The Samuel Rea Shops in Hollidaysburg see the bulk of the hopper car rebuilding program, with this photograph showing some of the welding operations. ***(Photo courtesy of Conrail)***

The formation of Conrail led to train routing which, it was hoped, would cut delivery schedules across the entire Northeast. This train, a Harrisburg-to-Bethlehem coal train with a consist from the Chessie System, is on ex-Reading rails in Bethlehem, Pa., but the power is ex-Erie-Lackawanna and Penn Central. ***(Photo by John Taibi)***

The winter of 1977 necessitated enormous digging-out operations all over Conrail and certainly did not help its financial woes. Here in New England, an eastbound freight snakes through the Berkshires at Washington, Mass., behind an SW-1500 switcher and three GP-9s. ***(Photo by Tom Hildreth)***

Above, a three-unit ex-Penn Central lashup heads an eastbound freight into the approach to Enola Yards near Harrisburg, Pa. Below, the mix of motive power on Conrail freights has never been more graphically demonstrated than in this crazy lashup. At the lead are two U-25Bs, both originally from the New York Central, one of which has been repainted in Conrail blue. The third unit is an ex-Erie-Lackawanna GP-35 renumbered into the Conrail roster, and the fourth is a Canadian National unit on lease. John Taibi took this photograph and the one on the opposite page. Here, in the Secaucus, N.J., terminal of the ex-Reading, sit locomotives from three of the consolidated roads at midnight.

3642
Reading
Lines
SOUTHERN

The stretch of ex-Pennsy main line west of Harrisburg is one part of Conrail where trainwatching is most fascinating, with the passage of everything imaginable. At top, a two-unit trailer train slams by westbound at Duncannon, Pa., with a work train headed eastbound. *(Photograph by John Gabriel)* Below, two eastbound freights wait to proceed into the Enola Yards, one with trailer train consists and an old blacked-out Penn Central SD-35 at the lead. An Erie Lackawanna GP-35 sits on the adjacent track.

6033
2566
2566

3646
ERIE-LACKAWANNA
3646
3616

The consolidation of railroads into Conrail enabled through freights to use all portions of the system to expedite shipment. Here, a train comes over the bridge at Iona Island across the New Jersey Division River Line on the west shore of the Hudson River. It has worked its way up from points in Pennsylvania and will end its run in Perlman Yards at Selkirk, N.Y. ***(Photo by John Taibi)***

There are two reasons why Conrail loses money on its operation: severe winters and unprofitable branch line operations. In 1978, a blizzard hit New England with record snowfall. Fighting through snow yields dramatic railroad photographs, but does little to soothe the nerves of the accountants. Here, Tom Hildreth captures, at top, an eight-unit lashup moving light through Chester, Mass., and headed by an experimental GE C-30. At bottom, a three-unit consist heads upgrade through Middlefield, Mass. *(Photo by Tom Hildreth)*

2721
2721
CONRAIL
2721

Tom Hildreth also has captured two scenes of a branch line operation that does little for Conrail's financial health, A once-a-week run of Contrail NW-2 along ex–New York Central single-track branch line to Ware, Mass., runs along the Ware River (side) and is greeted in Ware by four very young rail fans. This SW-1500 has yet to be repainted blue—or even get the ''CR'' stencil.

WARE LUMBER CO.
COMPLETE
BUILDING SUPPLIES
PENN CENTRAL
9557

Dick Herbert has captured the merged system in settings of mountains, yards, and rivers. Top left, a CNJ-EL combination at Elizabethport, N.J. Below, a PC and leased Chicago and North Western power combination near Newark, N.J. Top right, the four U-36Bs originally intended for Auto-Train but now painted in Conrail blue are shown on a winter day at Selkirk, N.Y. Bottom right, an Enola-bound freight heads over the Susquehanna River Bridge.

2971
CONRAIL
2971
CONRAIL

Above, a solid CN-leased power unit is shown with a freight at Port Jervis, N.Y. Left, a westbound freight comes over the scenic Hackensack River Bridge at Croxton, N.J. Upper right, a mixed E-L and RDG lashup at Arden, N.Y. Below, an E-L combo on a westbound freight at Hackensack, N.J.

SCL
3603
ERIE LACKAWANNA
ERIE LACKAWANNA

9248
2758
SOUTHERN
PACIFIC
9248

The operations of Conrail, despite the federal funds allocated to revive the deteriorated railroad facility, are still tied to the economy, and out of the economic set of constraints and opportunities Conrail must survive in the transportation marketplace. The challenge is very clear: Conrail must offer its shippers the most economical and advantageous means of moving commodities from shipper to destination. If labor costs go up, Conrail must find an operating solution to keep from passing these costs on to the shipper. If the weather deals a disastrous blow such as the snows and high winds of the winter of 1977, Conrail must not only absorb the costs of keeping the line open, but must also keep goods moving so that its customers do not have to shut down. In addition, Conrail must market more aggressively than the truckers, must keep its cargo intact so that losses—either through pilferage or derailment—do not occur.

Over 7700 miles of defective roadbed—the first cause of derailments—had to be attacked immediately. If the trains were not content to move slowly, they might all end up derailed in the ditch. The roadbed rebuilding program had progressed so well that by the spring of 1980, Amtrak, which uses Conrail in its east-west schedules, was able to announce schedule speedups for the first time in many years. Freight schedules were speeded up by as much as six hours, and the full benefits of the track rebuilding program are yet to be realized.

To combat the open looting of freight in yards, Conrail recruited a K-9 corps that almost immediately became effective, with 200 arrests reported throughout the system. The railroad will still continue to be the target for theft and vandalism, but "going to the dogs," as Conrail has done, will make the railroad yards an uneasy place for the criminal.

Conrail was not expected to turn losses into profits overnight. However, the rate of losses has been lowered. Barring some type of general economic failure in the Northeast, and with the ever-growing concern for energy conservation, the battered railroad system that once was the Penn Central and five other bankrupt roads might just become profitable. In the second quarter of 1979, Conrail's economic performance looked promising enough to where some viewers expected it to survive in the period 1980–1984 without any further Federal subsidy. Plans for partial dismemberment of Conrail into an Eastern and a Western division in the event the railroad faltered were put on the back shelf by USRA. The recession of 1980 might hurt Conrail—but with the Federal Government playing an increasingly greater role as the regulator of our total economy, who is to say what might happen. The need for a cohesive railroad system in the Northeast has been proven, and the rehabilitation of that system has been clearly demonstrated to have had a positive effect.

Above left, the Southern Pacific comes to Conrail. Below, an ex-New York Central F-7 leads a freight at Allentown, Pa.

A brand-new GP-40-2 heads westward past an old, abandoned way station near Enola, Pa. Conrail has ordered some 392 new locomotives since its inception, and these, together with the refurbished locomotives, have alleviated the power shortage.

Three six-axle locomotives pound westward with a Pennsylvania Power and Light Co. unit train, UFY669, at Newport, Pa. It is on a newly laid section of continuous welded rail, and John Taibi clocked it at better than 50 mph, a speed unheard of when the roadbed was in bad shape. The growing energy crisis and the return to coal-fired generation plants have given the unit train additional emphasis, and we should be seeing more of them in the years to come.

The smallest of the railroads to be merged into Conrail was the Lehigh and Hudson River Railroad. Above are three of the few locomotives acquired by Conrail on a run to Maybrook, N.Y. Upper right, another color scheme to enter Conrail land was the power on NE74, a pool train operated with the Burlington Northern. This power pool sometimes included locomotives of the Delaware and Hudson and the Norfolk and Western. *(Both photos by John Taibi.)* Below, a two-unit eastbound deadhead en route for Enola Yards meets a westbound freight.

2563
2563

5570

It seems hard to imagine that eventually, the Conrail refurbishment program will have all of its locomotives in the new blue colors of the road but, until then, here was the mix of color schemes in the year 1977. Top left, a three-unit Erie-Lackawanna consist heads a westbound freight through Port Jervis, N.Y., on the Ex–E-L main line. At bottom, the Canadian National comes to Conway, Pa., on this Conrail freight headed up the ex-Pennsy main line paralleling the Ohio River. Above, an aerial view of a Conrail trailer-train at Bear Mountain, N.Y.

Despite the electrification of the Pennsy routes from New York to Washington and westward to Harrisburg, an increasing volume of freight is now being powered by diesels. Rather than change to straight electrics, all run-through freight going from one non-electrified portion of the line to another retains the same locomotive. At left, an old Alco RS-11 and two RDS-12s haul an eastbound freight through Monmouth Junction, N.J. These units have since been retired and traded in for new locomotives.

An ex–New York Central GP-40, one of the first of this type built by EMD, is the trailing unit on this eastbound freight at Enola, Pa. As on all locomotives, the old logos have been blacked out and the "CR" initials have been applied, until it is due for its turn in the paint shop.

READING
9532
9551

Symbol freight NH-2 rolls through the town of Bancroft, Mass., powered by five SW-1500 switching-type locomotives. Only one of the units has been "CR'd"—the others are still in their old Penn Central markings. ***(Photo by Tom Hildreth)***

The "CR" process overlays all power types, regardless of their former owners. The famed Erie-Lackawanna logo is blacked out and the "CR" inserted, right in the middle of the diamond, on their freight coming over the bridge out of the Consolidated Yard at Allentown, Pa. *(Photo by John Gabriel)* Below, a brace of FL-9s—those locomotives capable of running under diesel power or straight electric, originally bought by the New Haven—come out of a tunnel at Oscawanna, N.Y., on their way to Harmon, N.Y., with a commuter run. *(Photo by John Taibi)*

Once upon a time, the 6145 wore the red keystone of the Pennsy on its nose; now it is the white CR. It is eastbound for Harrisburg, Pa., with a merchandise freight, and, from its position on #2 track east, it may well bypass the yards at Enola, going over the Rockville Bridge and on through the downtown Harrisburg area.

If Conrail can make it in terms of improved shipper schedules, it will be the fleet of TV (Trailer-Van) symbol freights that will be watched closely by customers and operating personnel alike. Above, a late-afternoon TV symbol freight heads westbound at a speed approaching 60 miles per hour at Maryville, Pa. Above right, John Taibi has photographed TV-10 racing through Metuchen, N.J., past a stationary freight that has stopped to switch cars in the Ford assembly plant there. The very essence of Conrail is highlighted by the John Taibi photograph at right below, with three Conrail SD-40-2s heading westbound through Newport, Pa., with TV-9. These are among the more recently delivered locomotives on the line, and the vanguard of the fleet of nearly 400 new units that has replaced much of the unserviceable power still on the system.

By 1978, nearly half of Conrail's freights operating in the electrified districts between Washington and Newark and Harrisburg to Philadelphia were running behind diesel power. As spring of 1980 came, Conrail had retired virtually every one of its classic GG-1's which had served for nearly a third of a century in freight service, and only the 5000-hp E-44's were left to pull freights under the wire. Because so many freights moved over formerly independent rail systems, it became easier to use diesel power exclusively than to switch power from electric to non-electric. The cost to maintain the GG-1's was another factor. Here a westbound freight crosses the Delaware River at Morrisville, Pa. At right, a three-unit combination starts its run northward out of Potomac Yard.

And miraculously, a second Nickel Plate Berkshire, #765, has now been brought back to life by the Fort Wayne Railroad Historical Society. With its members working up to their knees in rust and grime, the 2-8-4 was completely overhauled, and in late 1979—20 years after her fires had last gone dead—#765 sprang to life anew, clanking along at 50 mph over ex-NKP lines.

The 2101 proudly pulled the Chessie Steam Special excursion trains for two years, and then fate befell this proud locomotive. In March 1979, while stored at Chessie's Stevens Yard roundhouse in Silver Grove, Kentucky, it was gutted by a fire which swept through the roundhouse that also destroyed track machinery and GP-40 #4090.

2299
2299
2299

At left, ex-Pennsy and Reading power haul this westbound string of empties under the main passenger concourse at Trenton's Penn Central Station. Below, a pair of new SD-40-2s pass through Arlington, Va., en route inbound to Potomac Yard. The move to diesel power in the Northeast Corridor has brought out every type of diesel unit that Conrail operates.

6294 6294
2283 2283
ER

Harrisburg, Pa., is one of the centers of Conrail activity where trains may be seen constantly, from all sides and all directions. The yards at Enola are some of the busiest to be found anywhere, yet railroaders say that traffic has dropped from its former levels. The ex-Reading yards at Rutherford have been cleaned out of their former owner's power and furnished with ex-Pennsy locomotives. Railroaders there now complain that these locomotives have been badly maintained, despite Conrail's renewed emphasis on maintenance. At left, a string of ex-Pennsy locomotives heads westward into Rutherford Yards in late afternoon. At top is another late-afternoon scene west of Enola yards as three SD-45s, headed by an ex-Erie-Lackawanna unit, head east towards the giant yards.

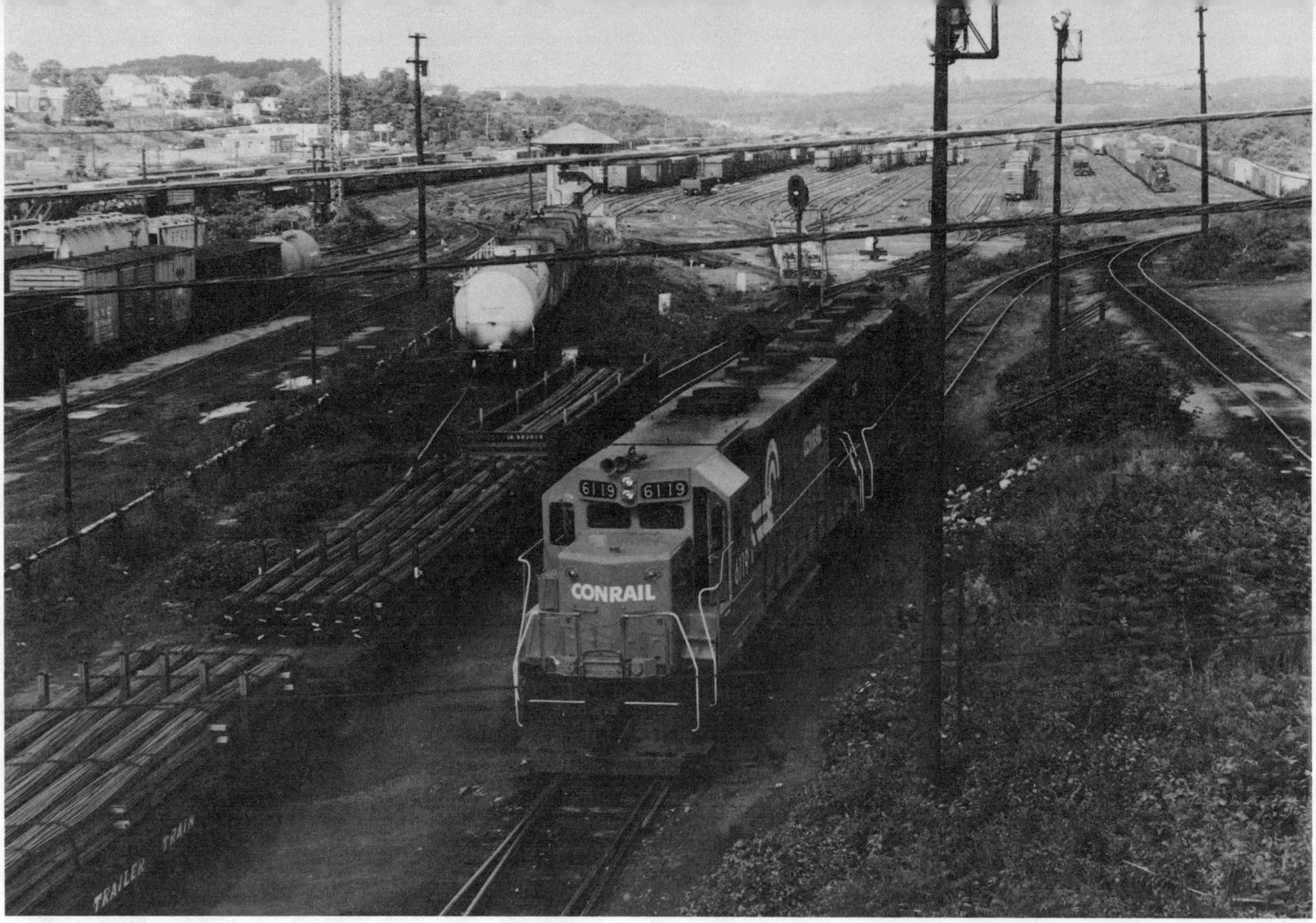
6119
6119
CONRAIL
TRAILER TRAIN

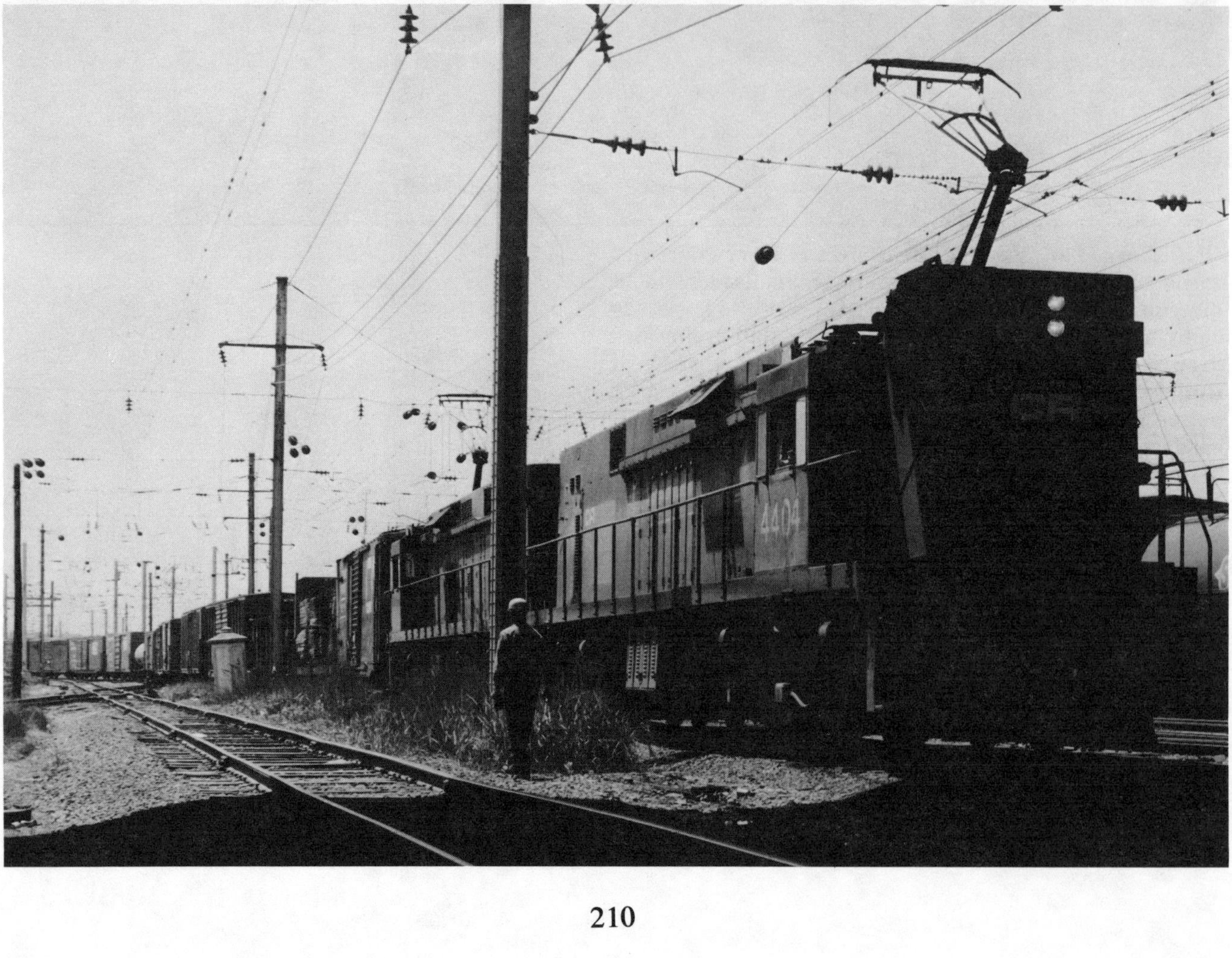
4404

And so the crisis of the railroad network in the Northeast has eased, by virtue of Federal intervention. The trains continue to roll, thanks to Conrail. At each quarter, Conrail reports a smaller and smaller loss, coupled with progress as well. The cost of the neglect of at least twenty years' worth of maintenance on a rail system over one hundred years old is still being felt, in dollars that must be spent to improve the service to a point where the operation will at least break even, and, if possible, make a profit. There are those critics of Conrail that still insist it can never be done. There are other critics that assail the federal funds being dumped into Conrail. But it is very clear that the nation's economy cannot survive very long if the entire railroad network in the Northeast has to stop operating. Conrail must succeed; the nation has no other choice, at least not under the free-enterprise system. Subsidization, or at least the extension of deep lines of credit, is a far better alternative than nationalizing the railroads.

5

A Look Behind . . . and a Look Ahead

Despite the jet age, despite the superhighways, and despite the most difficult period ever for some railroads, America's fascination with the train is still there. Railroading is something that has turned people on since the days of the first iron horse. It is dramatized in song, books have been written about its history and its operations, and the model railroading and toy train industries still enjoy profitable sales. And then there is that unique group called railfans that will brave the bitter cold of winter and the ninety-degree heat of summer just to come out either to watch or to photograph the trains. The mystique of the rails is indescribable; even the blast of a six-chime diesel airhorn can sometimes electrify the supposedly indifferent onlooker. The romance of the railroad era has been recaptured commercially in places such as the Victoria Station restaurants, which are built up using the sides of old boxcars and cabooses; and over half a hundred other dining establishments have been designed around the railroad motif. Many railroad museums exist, and whenever a special event of national significance arises, the train invariably becomes involved in it somehow. Yet, how many of the people who visit these locations will ride Amtrak rather than drive their car?

While the high-speed ground transportation program currently is concentrated on the Northeast Corridor Improvement Program, the interest of the rail fan still turns with nostalgia to that traditional symbol of the railroad, the Iron Horse. The wholesale conversion from steam to diesel had sent thousands upon thousands of steam locomotives to the scrap heap. However, there have been a few survivors. Today, these locomotives, given tender, loving care by trainmen who have not lost the skills of boilermaking and roundhouse repairs, come out for fan trips and other ceremonial occasions. Still other locomotives, not able to be fired up and run over the rails again, are enshrined in museums and other places where vandals cannot get to them.

Of the active steam locomotives, none is better known than the Southern Railway's #4501, a 2-8-2 Mikado that is used for fan trips all over the system. The star of the lot, however, is the Nickel Plate Berkshire #759, which during its active life hauled fast freight along the stretch of main line that paralleled the competing New York Central from Cleveland to Buffalo. The 759 is quartered in Steamtown, U.S.A., in Bellows Falls, Vermont, but every so often it is fired up and sent out on fan trips as far west as Chicago. Whenever it operates on the Norfolk and Western's line that now is the successor to the Nickel Plate, memories rise anew. And miraculously, a second Nickel Plate Berkshire, #765, has now been brought back to life by the Fort Wayne Railroad Historical Society. With its members working up to their knees in rust and grime, the 2-8-4 was completely overhauled, and in late 1979—20 years after her fires had last gone dead—#765 sprang to life anew, clanking along at 50 mph over ex-NKP lines.

The Reading Railroad also had a classic locomotive, the 2102. It also escaped the cutting torch to become the famed Number 1 that pulled the Freedom Train on its Bicentennial tour. Its sister locomotive, the 2101, was repainted in the yellow, orange, and blue of the Chessie System. The 2101 proudly pulled the Chessie Steam Special excursion trains for two years, and then fate befell this proud locomotive. In March 1979, while stored at Chessie's Stevens Yard roundhouse in Silver Grove, Kentucky, it was gutted by a fire which swept through the roundhouse that also destroyed track machinery and GP-40 #4090. The fate of the 2101 was in doubt until a swap was made. The 2101 would be restored to its American Freedom Train exterior and put on permanent display at the B&O Railroad Museum in Baltimore. In return, the B&O Museum would give up a massive C&O 4-8-4 locomotive, the 614, which had spent nearly 30 years in storage and on display at Baltimore. The Western Maryland roundhouse at Hagerstown, Maryland, soon had a new occupant—the 614—and the Steam Locomotive Corporation of America went to work. By the fall of 1980, the 614 could be fired up, and like the 765 of the Nickel Plate, spring back to life.

Everywhere these locomotives went, they brought back the memories of the steam engine to those long familiar with them. And to those born long after the diesels took over, it was like seeing a bit of history flash by. It was small wonder that people from all walks of life became boilermakers, steamfitters, mechanics, and ironsmiths in their spare time to bring these giants of steam back to life.

The railroads remembered their history, because they played such a major part in it. When it came time for the United States to celebrate its two hundredth birthday, the railroads commemorated the event by running special trains and by repainting locomotives in a brilliant array of red, white, and blue, especially those units that were numbered 1776 or 1976. The resultant display of colors from each of the railroads is something which we will not see again—until, of course, our nation reaches its three hundredth birthday.

What of the future? The Department of Transportation's high-speed test track at Pueblo, Colo., may hold some of the answers, such as the tracked, air-cushion vehicle. The high-speed ground transportation project in the Northeast Corridor Improvement Program may hold other answers. Whatever the timing for these future events, it will be inexorably linked to the nation's energy supply, which is being depleted at an ever-increasing rate.

The Southern 4501 sits for a portrait with banners and polished brightwork on a June 1975 fan trip in the Louisville, Ky., area. *(Photo by Leonard J. Dunman)* Below, the DOT Tracked Air Cushion Vehicle sits on its test track at Pueblo, Colo. *(Photo courtesy of DOT)*

The Bicentennial was the occasion for the railroads to dig into their paint lockers to come up with every type of variation of the red, white, and blue stars-and-stripes colors for their locomotives and oftentimes their rolling stock. There is perhaps no industry that has affected the growth of the country more than the railroads, and, as a result, the railroads were among the foremost to observe the nation's Bicentennial celebration. The array of color schemes was as different as the railroads themselves. If there was a locomotive on the roster numbered 1976, 1776, 776, or anything with a 76 in it, this would be the one selected to get the star-spangled treatment. Many times, the railroads would run a Bicentennial Special to some landmark of the nation's Revolution or progress, and these brilliantly painted locomotives would be the ones to haul it. Even the small switching roads and little industrial railroads managed to paint one of their locomotives in red, white, and blue.

1776
Norfolk and Western
NW 1776
UP 171263
UNION PACIFIC

SOUTHERN PACIFIC
3197
SPIRIT of '76
SP

Above, Conrail's Bicentennial Express at Suffern, N.Y., on the morning of July 4, 1976. At right, a posed shot with the Erie-Lackawanna Bicentennial units and the Delaware and Hudson 1776 at Starucca Viaduct in New York. The Delaware and Hudson converted a second locomotive to Bicentennial colors, and this appears below.

ERIE LACKAWANNA
3632
1776

1976
Delaware & Hudson
Spirit of Freedom
1976

Conrail repainted one of its legendary GG-1s, the 4800, in Bicentennial colors; it is seen with two other GG-1s heading south from Newark, N.J. The 4800 was subsequently repainted in Conrail blue, and "Old Rivets"—as it was called by its crews—was finally retired in late 1979 as part of the entire GG-1 fleet of freight locomotives. It was purchased from Conrail for $30,000 by the National Railway Historical Society and taken to Strasburg, Pennsylvania at the Railroad Museum of Pennsylvania. Permanently enshrined there, it will be repainted in the pinstripes and lettering of its original owner, the Pennsylvania Railroad.

The New York, Ontario, and Western used a brilliant red, white, and blue scheme for its locomotive, seen at middle opposite page. Below, the Pittsburgh and Lake Erie, now completely divorced from the Penn Central, has painted its 1501 in red and white stripes, and it is shown at Monaca, Pa., on a commuter run. ***(All photos are by Dick Herbert)***

1776
1776

At left, a Bicentennial Excursion operated by the Delaware and Hudson rolls through Sidney, N.Y., on the weekend of April 24-25, 1976. During the Bicentennial year, the railroads ran frequent excursions and fan trips to many places that commemorated the nation's most historic moments. *(Photo by John Taibi)* Above, another number 1776, this one owned by the Detroit, Toledo, and Ironton, poses at Flat Rock, Michigan. *(Photo by Howard Ameling)*

From the mighty Southern Pacific to the tiny Ohio Lime Company, the Bicentennial paint jobs proliferated. Above, another Southern Pacific unit, the 6800, sits in star-spangled paint at Oakland, Ca. Below, the Ohio Lime Company has painted a fifty-ton Plymouth diesel switcher in red, white, and blue. *(Both photos courtesy of Howard Ameling)*

The Steam Engine Lives On . . . .

Despite the presence of the diesel as the mainstay of American railroading, there is perhaps nothing as mind-blowing as the sight of a huge steam locomotive, perhaps the most modern of its era, charging down the track, cylinders and rods flying and smoke belching from its stack. This was the way railroading had been for well over a hundred years, and even those that had never seen a steam locomotive in action were enthralled by the few survivors of the technological revolution. These steamers are used for excursions and fan trips which are usually sold out weeks in advance of their announcement. Rail fans come with still cameras, movie sound cameras, tape recorders, and anything else they can haul just to record the sights and sounds of the Iron Horse.

Not only was the Iron Horse used for fan trips. Several little railroads, motivated by this same nostalgia, managed to capture steam locomotives that had been in hiding for two decades or more and restore them to revenue service. The Crab Orchard and Egyptian Railroad, a little 8.5-mile railroad running from Crainville to Marion, Illinois, captured two steam locomotives, a 2-4-2 saddle-tanker, and a 2-8-0 Consolidation. It is possibly the only railroad in existence that hauls a tiny fleet of piggyback trailer-vans behind steam.

Winding down the Cuyahoga River valley on a 27-mile course from Cleveland to Akron, Ohio, is the Cuyahoga Valley Line. On it steams a 1918-vintage USRA 2-8-2 Mikado, #4070, acquired from the Grand Trunk Western. Six hundred twenty-five such locomotives were built by government order, and 25 each were bought by the GTW and the New York Central. The 4070 was retired in 1960, and purchased by railfans, thereby saving it from the cutting torch. The Midwest Railway Historical Foundation now owns and maintains the locomotive and its 13 passenger cars, and steam excursions now run regularly during the summer. Like all such preservation efforts, it depends upon volunteer effort and contributions, and there is always the possibility that such railroad nostalgia could be shut down due to increased operating costs in this inflationary economy.

It is regrettable that some of the most classic steam locomotives are extinct. The famous Pennsy K-4 Pacific sits as a monument on the Horseshoe Curve near Altoona. Every one of the great locomotives of the New York Central went to the scrap heap without a single survivor. Ditto for the hillclimbers of the Norfolk and Western, the Southern Pacific, and the Baltimore and Ohio. What has been preserved is indeed a tribute to some farsighted individuals who realized that one day remembrance would be something vital.

302

At left, the Reading 2102 puts down a cloud of smoke as it approaches the overpass near Deposit, N.Y., with a fan trip. John Taibi took this photograph. Above, a Boston and Maine Pacific sits in Steamtown, U.S.A., in Vermont. ***(Photograph Courtesy of Howard Ameling)***

The Reading 4-8-4s wore two costumes. The 2102 pulled the Freedom Train, and became Number 1 for this duty. Its sister locomotive, the 2101, was brought over to the Chessie System, where it was painted the yellow and blue colors of the railroad and sent out on fan trips. The 2102 with the Freedom Train is pictured at Croxton Yard, while the 2101 in Chessie colors is shown at Baltimore, Md. ***(Both photos by Dick Herbert)***

Although Conrail took over all operations of the Penn Central, a bit of sentimentality, plus the power of a concerted rail fan group, resulted in the restoration of GG-1 #4935 back to the olive drab and yellow pinstripes of the Pennsylvania Railroad, its original colors, which it had worn nearly forty years ago. It has been that long since these Raymond Loewy-styled locomotives were first delivered to the Pennsy, and it is only now that most of these classic locomotives are being retired. Conrail has already retired its GG-1 fleet, and Amtrak will retire what GG-1 survivors are left, once it takes delivery of the new AEM-7 "Mighty Mouse." But here we have the 4935 as a working reminder of the finest electric locomotive ever to operate on American railroads.

Perhaps the steam counterpart to the GG-1 for appearance, reliability, and performance was the Nickel Plate Road series of Berkshires which raced freight along the banks of Lake Erie at speeds approaching those of passenger trains. These Berkshires competed head-to-head with the Niagaras and Mohawks of the New York Central, and most of the time they won. Of these locomotives, the 759 and 765 were retired, but somehow never scrapped. The 759 now belongs to Steamtown, U.S.A., and is considered by many to be the queen of the steam excursion locomotives. John Taibi photographed the 759 at Hancock, N.Y., running westward on the Erie-Lackawanna.

The Steamtown excursions are not limited to the 759. Below, a doubleheaded consist of ex-Boston and Maine light Pacifics heads through western Massachusetts, as captured by Tom Hildreth. Opposite, running late and drawing expectant crowds everywhere the 2101, dressed up as the Chessie Steam Special, races westward through Rockville, Md. Each of its sixteen cars was crammed with railfans on a spring excursion to Harpers Ferry, W. Va. The 2101 was subsequently gutted by a roundhouse fire in March 1979.

2101
2101
2101
Chessie STEAM SPECIAL

While the 759 is the queen of excursion locomotives, the Southern 4501 is perhaps the most widely seen of the steam locomotives today. Kept in perfect running condition by the Southern, the 4501 has visited perhaps the entire eastern portion of the country. It runs every year through most of the Southern's territory. At left, the 4501 is on the Norfolk and Western line at Norwalk, Ohio, on an excursion train from Roanoke to Chicago. Above, the 4501 rolls through Bellevue, Ohio, with another excursion special. ***(Both photos by Howard Ameling)***

In some instances, steam locomotives are undergoing complete rebuilding by historical landmark groups whose desire to preserve the past matches their mechanical ability. In these three photographs by Leonard Dunman, a 1905 vintage Louisville and Nashville 4-6-2 is shown on the opposite pages in its dismantled state; below, as it looked about three years ago, before the activation project. It is owned by the Kentucky Railway Museum, which decided the 152 would be a fan trip locomotive of the 1980s.

Not only the steam locomotive was the subject of fan trips and preservation—the old commuter cars also were finding their historical niche. John Gabriel photographed the Reading green MU cars running on a fan trip sponsored by the Philadelphia Chapter of the National Railway Historical Society. They are 46 years old.

The railroad station is perhaps the second most visible landmark of railroading, after the steam locomotive. Regrettably, many architecturally great landmarks were demolished when the passenger train passed out of existence on many roads. Many others were boarded up and daily survive the test of aging, the vandals, and the threat of demolition. There is a growing movement for reusing such railroad stations, and it has become the pet project of many planners and urbanologists that feel the old depot may be worth preserving after all. Here in Louisville is the castlelike railroad station on a rainy day in October 1976. ***(Photo by Leonard Dunman)***

Even the diesel locomotive is enshrined in railroad history. The American Locomotive Company developed the PA-1, a passenger diesel which was one of the most aesthetic but not the most widely sold of units. In the elimination of passenger trains on most railroads, the PA-1 also became extinct, except for four surviving units, the famed numbers 51 through 54 of the Santa Fe. These were likewise ready to be scrapped until the Delaware and Hudson interceded and bought the units. They were repainted, refurbished, and renumbered 16 through 19. They were used in light freight service until the Massachusetts Bay Transit Authority needed power for its commuter service, and the D&H leased them to MBTA. The PA-1's have been subsequently replaced by new MBTA F40PHR locomotives.

And the Future?

On the other end of the line are the futuristic concepts being tried out for surface transportation. These are research and development ideas which today are beyond the means or interest of the operating railroads. They include advanced propulsion systems and a guideway system other than the traditional steel rails spaced 4 feet 8½ inches apart. In the test tract at Pueblo, Colo., the Office of High Speed Ground Transportation has been studying these concepts ever since the early 1970s. The objective is to develop a workable means of moving people at ground level at high speeds, both in intercity transport and for commuter transportation.

However, such an alternative will have to show a clear superiority over the automobile as the prime mover of people. This is the heart of the problem that DOT faces. America has had a greater love affair with the automobile than any other type of transport. Thus, speed, convenience, comfort, and cost are all factors to be considered as far as the high-speed ground transportation program is concerned.

Other countries have developed passenger trains that travel at sustained speeds of over 120 miles per hour. This is feasible here in the United States right now, with both Metroliner and the French or Rohr Turboliners. However, a massive job has to be done to curves and grade crossings to ensure the safety of the line, and this is being attempted in the Northeast Corridor Improvement Project. The advanced concepts such as Tracked Air Cushion Vehicles—these are still in the laboratory stage, for the most part. Some day, they will be a part of our future—but not very soon.

Above, a model of the Tracked Air Cushion Vehicle (TACV) sits in a laboratory at the High Speed Ground Transportation test site in Pueblo, Colo. An operating model sits in a test track at the Pueblo site. Above right, a Linear Induction Motor Test Vehicle sits on its test track. Below, an aerial view of the Pueblo test site. ***(All photographs courtesy of the Department of Transportation)***

DEPARTMENT OF TRANSPORTATION
OFFICE OF HIGH SPEED GROUND TRANSPORTATION
THE GARRETT CORPORATION

An artist's rendering of an urban commuter type of TACV, capable of speeds of up to 160 miles per hour. ***(Photo courtesy of the Department of Transportation)***

In Conclusion . . .

We have seen the emergence of Amtrak, Auto-Train, and Conrail in the past ten years, born either out of desperation or out of the idea that there is a better way of operating the railroads. Whatever the reasons for these new railroads, all of them arose in response to the needs of both passengers and businessmen. We have seen that without the railroads there would be wholesale chaos and disruption of the American economy. But, at the same time, we have also seen that inadequate management, inflexible labor, unfair regulation, and lack of imagination can make the railroads a necessary evil instead of an asset to the American way of life. We have also seen that, unless these new railroads work, the answer is nationalization of the rail system—something nobody wants.

What the future holds remains to be seen. Conrail continues to make slow progress—but, it is hoped, not too slow for the deadline of its federal mandate. The Chessie System and the Norfolk and Western continue to exist as profitable railroads, despite labor problems. The Chessie System is currently in active merger negotiations with the Seaboard Coast Line–Louisville and Nashville combination known as the Family Lines. If completed, this will create a huge end-to-end railway network covering the entire eastern half of the country, from the northern tip of Michigan down to the Gulf of Mexico. The Norfolk and Western demonstrated how a railroad could operate without featherbedding-type work rules. Operating like the Florida East Coast Railroad, the N&W ran trains during an 82-day strike period in 1978-1979 with two-man crews, 250-mile days, and no caboose at the rear of its trains. With a stripped-down labor force culled from the ranks of management (and even including secretaries), 275 trains per day were operated, compared to the 475 trains per day that the normal union-represented labor force was able to move.

Other profitable railroads are now either looking to merge, and two railroads have not been successful in remaining intact. West of the Mississippi the railroad empire of the Burlington Northern was increased still further by its merger with the Frisco Lines, and its current operational outlook has as its theme, the movement of coal all throughout the newly emerging rail corridors running out of Wyoming, Nebraska, and other Western states. The Santa Fe is now talking about merging with its long-time competitor, the Southern Pacific, which has forgotten altogether about its previous merger ideas with the Family Lines. Other railroads are actively looking for merger partners in efforts to reduce duplicative route competition or to create larger end-to-end networks.

The Rock Island and the Milwaukee Road were two of the unfortunates that could not find successful merger partners, or unlike the hapless Penn Central, were not blessed by a Federally guaranteed solution to their debt crises. The Rock's difficulties extended back to its third bankruptcy. A projected merger with the Union Pacific died when the Interstate Commerce Commission refused to act. The Carter

Administration did not aid the Rock when it took a disastrous strike. Where the Norfolk and Western was successful in emulating the Florida East Coast Railroad in operating with reduced crews and realistic work rules, the Rock was prohibited by the ICC from a similar operation. Finally, the 7000-mile, 13-state railroad was pronounced dead in January 1980, and is currently parceled out to 17 railroads, with about 65% of track and 88% of its traffic now maintained by these railroads. Nonetheless, some substantial segments of main line have been shut down, serving locations such as Des Moines, Iowa and Fort Worth, Texas.

The Milwaukee Road, also in financial straits, is being reduced from a 9800-mile system to about a 3400-mile property. Sometimes called "Milwaukee II," or "The New Milwaukee," the exact definition of the new line was unclear as of June, 1980. The inclination is that most of the property west of Miles City, Montana may go to other railroads, most likely the ever-growing Burlington Northern.

Amtrak is faced with a general reduction in service, but the infusion of new federal funds estimated at $631 million in Fiscal Year 1980 and $675 million in Fiscal Year 1981 may help to avert this. Amtrak is still recovering from the necessity of ordering new locomotives to replace the SDP-40F, which caused all sorts of problems. The question remains, will Amfleet replace the family car for intercity travel? Further, will Auto-Train continue to be viable in the face of losses? Its deal with Eastern Airlines to haul the passengers while Auto-Train hauls their automobiles may be very vulnerable to further rate cuts by car rental agencies. The concept of Auto-Train service is too good to compromise it. What really might be needed is another look at the placement of Auto-Train's terminals, and the feasibility of picking up passengers at many places along the gathering points to Florida.

In all fairness to the railroad passenger service effort, the progressive deterioration of the physical plant of the railroad may have caused Amtrak to receive more blame than it deserves. Amtrak just cannot haul passengers at convenient speeds, and, where this was felt to be critical, a multi-billion-dollar Northeast Corridor Improvement Project was put into effect. But compare what is now to what once was. In the 1950s, the New York Central operated a well-maintained, four-track main line from New York to Albany to Buffalo to Chicago. The *Twentieth Century Limited* operated over this 961-mile stretch in eighteen hours, leaving New York at 4:30 P.M. in the evening and arriving in Chicago at 9:30 A.M., Central Standard Time. By contrast, Amtrak's *Lake Shore Limited* leaves New York at 6:30 P.M., but does not arrive in Chicago until 2:55 P.M., Central Standard Time! This is nothing for Amtrak to be ashamed of, because this entire stretch of railroad line had two tracks removed by the New York Central in the interests of economy, and the remaining two tracks subsequently were left to rot by its successor, the Penn Central. The once-proud Water Level Route now must support a handful of Amtrak runs, and in addition must be rebuilt by Conrail to a point where it can attract and maintain freight business. This example typifies the challenges faced both by Amtrak, in its effort to establish long-distance passenger service, and by Conrail, in its effort to restore railroading operations to a system that almost stopped running.

The Federal Government is unquestionably becoming a major stockholder in the railroad business, because it is an unchallenged fact that the Government has a huge monetary investment in American railroading. It has become an increasingly active partner in the industry. There is little other choice, as we have seen exemplified by the near-collapse of the Penn Central. The dismemberment of the Rock Island and the Milwaukee Road might well serve as a deadly example of what happens when aid comes too late—or never comes at all.

In addition to the monetary aspects, there is also a national emergency aspect as well. In a news documentary shown on ABC's program, *20/20,* in June 1980, there was portrayed in shocking terms, the impact of hazardous materials shipments on railroads whose tracks have deteriorated and whose rolling stock was considered unsafe. Although the railroads have made progress in the repair of roadbeds and the installation of safety equipment such as headshields in tank cars, the program of modernization was considered to be too little and too late. Discounting the usual sensationalism of the TV media, the fact is inescapable that the Federal Government—in particular, the Federal Railroad Administration—needs far more enforcing powers and a far greater information systems resource than it presently has. The proliferation of highly dangerous cargoes on our rails, moving at high speeds over roadbeds which have only just begun to be renovated, could cause a potential catastrophic disaster to occur. What is required is money—lots of it—to hasten the repair of track and rolling stock, and to make sure there is an effective agency to both prevent such disasters from occuring, and to minimize the threat to life and environment once a derailment and accident has occurred.

Possibly, this is the reason why the Carter Administration, in the Spring of 1980, authorized an additional $750 million for the completion of the Northeast Corridor Improvement Project and the continuation of freight services along the lines of the now-dismembered Rock Island. While President Carter spoke in the Rose Garden about, "the very bright" future for rail transportation in the United States, and added, "Americans sometimes forget that trains are the transportation of the future, not the past," the President may well have included himself amongst the ranks of the forgetful. It was he, that during the fuel crisis of 1979, urged that there be a 43% cutback in Amtrak operation, and subsequently made a fast turnabout when it was discovered that Amtrak could hardly keep up with the surge of new passengers brought on by scarce and eventually very costly gasoline.

From the railroad enthusiast's standpoint, however, what happens in Washington, as well as in the front offices of these and other railroads across the nation is far removed from the feeling of excitement whenever a pounding freight roars over a grade crossing or whenever Amtrak comes gliding over the historic bridge at Harper's Feery to stop at the rustic station. These are sights sounds that will not go away, no matter what changes are made in the front office.

Perhaps the best place to feel this is at a spot along the Richmond, Fredericksburg, and Potomac just north of Crystal City in Arlington, Va. There, one can stand along the tracks and see the jets swoop in low on their landing pattern into National Airport. He can see the skyline and, at twilight, the lights of the Capitol, the Washington Monument, and many of the other government buildings. One scene echoes the roar and noise of the jet age. The other represents big government, always present, wherever we are and whatever we do. But as one looks down the tracks and hears the low drone of diesel engines and the high-pitched whine of superchargers on a northbound Chessie freight easing out of Potomac Yards, all of this is forgotten. It is like another world out there, as a trio of yellow, orange, and blue GP-40s glides by with over 100 cars of northbound freight. No wonder railroaders never wander far from their jobs, and a lot of others wish they could be up in that locomotive cab. The lure of the rails will be with some of us, most likely, for a long time to come.

Index